# Fit Pregnancy

Namita Jain is a clinical fitness specialist with the Bombay Hospital. Her career in the wellness space spans over 25 years and she holds prestigious international certifications in numerous health-related disciplines. Her company Live Active and brand Jaldi Fit are rapidly growing names in health and lifestyle products and services. Her latest association is with Diet Mantra, a pan-India venture, where she trains dieticians in the art of healthy eating for a healthy life and offers personalized weight management solutions.

Namita has written for leading newspapers and magazines on nutrition, fitness and health-related issues, and has authored several books, including *Jaldi Fit with Namita Jain, Jaldi Fit Kids, The Four Week Countdown Diet, Figure It Out* and *Sexy at Sixty*.

For more information on Namita and her wellness programmes, visit her websites www.liveactive.com and www.jaldifit.com.

## Also by Namita Jain

*Jaldi Fit with Namita Jain*

*Jaldi Fit Kids*

*Figure It Out*

*The Four Week Countdown Diet*

*Sexy at Sixty*

# Fit Pregnancy

## The Complete Health Plan for You and Your Baby

NAMITA JAIN

*Foreword by*
DR R.P. SOONAWALA

**Collins**
*An Imprint of* HarperCollins *Publishers*

First published in India in 2012 by Collins
An imprint of HarperCollins *Publishers*

Copyright © Namita Jain 2012

P- ISBN: 978-93-5029-344-7
E- ISBN: 978-93-5029-929-6

2 4 6 8 10 9 7 5 3

Namita Jain asserts the moral right to be identified
as the author of this work.

Illustrations by Ramakant Kamble

**HarperCollins *Publishers***
A-75, Sector 57, NOIDA, Uttar Pradesh  201301, India
77-85 Fulham Palace Road, London W6 8JB, United Kingdom
Hazelton Lanes, 55 Avenue Road, Suite 2900, Toronto, Ontario M5R 3L2
*and* 1995 Markham Road, Scarborough, Ontario M1B 5M8, Canada
25 Ryde Road, Pymble, Sydney, NSW 2073, Australia
195 Broadway, New York, NY 10007, USA

Typeset in 10/14 Mercury Display
Jojy Philip New Delhi 110 015

Printed and bound at
Thomson Press (India) Ltd.

# Contents

# Foreword

I have treated thousands of pregnant women over the last several decades. It has been an honour and a privilege to be doctor, friend and confidante to my clients in this, their most vulnerable yet miraculous time of their life.

In my experience, most pregnant women need a little handholding to remain fit during pregnancy. Some guidance, a feeling that they are not alone – that others, including their husband, share their turmoil, their emotional and physical upheavals.

Namita Jain, a certified lifestyle and health management specialist, provides all this and more in this book. She packs in a punch and covers topics that concern every pregnant woman's well-being. She advises on diet during pregnancy, a subject that has perplexed women since time immemorial. What should a woman eat during pregnancy? What kind of food is good for her and her baby? How much should she eat and how?

Her 'Square Meal' mantra, where the four sides of a square represent the four vital food groups that are essential for a well-balanced diet, is simply and succinctly explained. I strongly recommend that it be adopted by everybody, pregnant or otherwise.

*Fit Pregnancy* even answers the numerous questions we gynaecologists are constantly asked. It addresses common concerns during pregnancy – everything from mood swings and heartburn to back pain and round ligament pain. Namita suggests simple yet effective ways to deal with them, based on her clients' experiences and actual case studies.

She has devoted an entire segment to exercise of both body and mind, using her experience in this field to demonstrate exercise safety and benefits. She suggests tried and tested exercises for the nine months of pregnancy. She stresses, as I do to all my clients, that you must enjoy this wonderful time in your life and in nine months you are going to witness perhaps the greatest miracle of mankind – the birth of your baby.

In my opinion, *Fit Pregnancy* is one of the most comprehensive books on all things related to pregnancy. It is a must-have if you are pregnant or planning a baby.

Dr Rustom Phiroze Soonawala
Padma Shri – MD, FRCS, FRCOG, FICOG

# Congratulations,
# you're going to be a mother!

From here on, life as you know it will never be the same again. You will experience euphoria along with some trepidation. Right now you have more questions than answers. How do I stay healthy? How do I ensure that my baby is healthy? How can I have a normal delivery?

I am going to hold your hand and guide you through your rough and smooth times, making sure you and your baby get the best advice there is.

This book contains simple, hands-on suggestions that can be easily integrated into your lifestyle. Be prepared to be amazed at how quickly your body begins to respond. Not just on the outside, but also on the inside. Get ready to get super fit. So that when your baby arrives you are brimming with joy and good health.

Here's to a fit, safe and – dare I say it – enjoyable pregnancy!

# WEIGHT GAIN

Rich, fatty foods are like destiny:
They too shape our ends.

— Anonymous

# Weight Watch
## Gaining Weight during Pregnancy

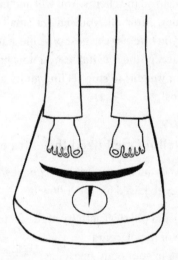

Women the world over have a common grouse – we're hardly ever happy with our weight, whether we're pregnant or not. Years of brainwashing by films, television and advertising have left an indelible mark on us.

Some women are scared to get pregnant for fear that they will not get back their original figure and keep putting off the decision to have a baby.

Take the case of my client Yasmin, a mother of three.

'I gained a lot of weight during my first pregnancy. I felt so self-conscious and miserable about my body that I didn't appreciate the miracle that was taking place. The second time around I was determined to make the most of it. I heeded the advice I was given, ate healthy and didn't put on excess weight. I enjoyed it so much that I decided to go for baby number three. The important thing is to feel good and happy about your pregnancy and eat healthy, fresh food regularly.'

I applaud Yasmin's pragmatic outlook and hold her as a shining example to all my clients. You will and must gain weight during pregnancy. After all, you have a small being growing inside you and you owe her the best possible start in life.

My advice: accept the inevitable. You now have a legitimate reason to put on weight, so stop feeling guilty and enjoy piling on the extra kilos!

## People keep telling me I need the extra energy. Why?

Your energy needs increase during pregnancy because of the additional energy required for the following:

✓ The growth and physical activity of the foetus
✓ The growth of the placenta
✓ The increase in your body size
✓ The additional work involved in carrying the weight of the foetus and extra maternal tissues
✓ The slow but steady rise in basal metabolic rate during pregnancy

So, here comes the question that's on all your minds...

## How much weight should I put on?

In a healthy pregnancy, experts recommend a weight gain of about 11 to 14 kg.

During the first trimester you may put on 1 to 2 kg. You may even lose up to 2 kg as a result of morning sickness. Do not get anxious about the weight loss or gain and try and eat 6 to 8 small meals through the day to keep up your strength. Drink plenty of fluids to make up for the loss of fluids that takes place when you vomit. Your baby will be nourished with all the nutrients you have accumulated before conception.

During the second trimester most women put on about 1 to 2 kg per month and during the third trimester you could gain about 2 to 3 kg per month, because your baby is growing rapidly.

Women who are underweight at the start of their pregnancy need to gain more weight than women who are overweight. The recommended weight gain for women carrying a single baby:

✓ Women who are close to their normal weight: 11 to 14 kg
✓ Overweight women: 7 to 11.5 kg
✓ Underweight women: 12.5 to 18 kg

## How much is too much? And how little is too little?

The ideal weight gain during pregnancy will vary from woman to woman. This is because of differences in height, weight, physical activity and metabolism. Your gynaecologist can help you determine a target that is right for your body, your health status and your pregnancy.

Pre-existing health conditions like diabetes may influence how much weight you are able to put on during your pregnancy.

Certain genetic factors may also play a role in determining how big you get.

Eating more calories than you and your baby need is not only unnecessary, it is not smart, and can lead to excessive weight gain. Eating too few calories, on the other hand, is potentially dangerous. As the pregnancy progresses, women who don't consume enough calories during their second and third trimester can seriously hamper the growth of their babies.

## Where does the weight go?

The weight is accounted for by the pregnancy and the resulting changes in you.

Healthy weight gain distribution is 1 to 2 kg in the first 13 weeks. After 13 weeks, you should ideally gain 2 kg per month, till delivery.

| Distribution of weight | kg |
|---|---|
| Baby | 2.5–3.5 |
| Placenta | 0.5–0.6 |
| Amniotic fluid | 1.0 |
| Uterus | 1.0 |
| Increased body fluid | 3.6 |
| Increased body fat, breast tissue | 3.2 |

Less than half the total weight you gain will reside in the foetus, placenta and amniotic fluid; the rest is accumulated in the breast tissues, fluid, blood and maternal stores, which are largely composed of body fat. This is where you will draw your resources from when you're breast feeding.

## How do I know I am gaining the right amount of weight?

Every woman's metabolism is different, so no two women will put on weight in the same way. But adopting good eating habits now will help you gain the amount of weight that is healthiest for you and your baby, and also keep you healthy for life.

My tips for healthy eating:

✓   Eat when you are hungry
✓   Eat small portions
✓   Snack healthy
✓   Don't overeat
✓   Get regular exercise

On average, you require 300 extra calories a day. As your pregnancy progresses, your appetite naturally guides you to take in the right amount of calories for you and your growing baby. Follow my 'Square Meal' diet guidelines for healthy eating habits to last you a lifetime.

### Excess weight gain

'I stuffed my face every chance I got. I couldn't resist the pure ghee laddoos my ma-in-law sent me. I put on 22 kg! My gynaecologist put me on a diet in my ninth month.'

Alas, we all know how easy it is to put on weight, especially when mothers and mothers-in-law come bearing mouth-watering gifts. But you should be aware that mothers-to-be who start off overweight or gain excess weight can have difficult deliveries. Excess weight can be hard on your baby too. Other pregnancy complications in women who gain excess weight include gestational diabetes, unsuccessful induction of labour, lacerations of the birth canal and cesarean section.

**A word of caution**

Sometimes excess weight gain is all water retention. Look for telltale signs – swollen hands and feet, or weight gain of more than 2 to 3 kg a week. But don't be alarmed, the swelling itself won't harm your foetus; in fact you will pee out excess fluid within a few weeks of delivery. Sometimes severe water retention can be a sign of a serious pregnancy complication called pre-eclampsia, occurring in late pregnancy, which requires immediate medical attention.

'I am anxious about becoming too fat and never getting back to normal again. How do I control putting on excess weight?'

This is something most of my clients worry about. You're right, the main problem with gaining too much weight is that it may be difficult to lose after the baby is born. But it is important to remember that excess weight gain is not usually a medical problem. Of course, you need to eat when you are hungry, but try to decrease the quantity and substitute low-fat foods for high-fat ones – so have skimmed milk instead of full cream and frozen yoghurt instead of ice-cream.

Here are my suggestions to avoid gaining excess weight:

✓ Eat before you get hunger pangs. Hunger pangs can make you binge on unhealthy food.

✓ Eat regularly – 6 to 8 meals a day.

✓ Don't eat when stressed; take a walk or chew gum instead.

✓ Eat slowly and savour each bite.

✓ If you are a compulsive eater, snack on bean sprouts, boiled potatoes, carrots, cucumber, fruit and channa.

✓ At meal times, serve yourself once generously – avoid seconds.

✓ Avoid fried food and dessert.

✓ Drink water instead of cold drinks which contain lots of sugar.

## Poor weight gain

'I have always had a problem gaining weight... I'm worried that I won't gain enough now that I'm pregnant.'

You're right to be concerned. Poor weight gain increases the possibility that your baby will not get adequate nutrition or develop properly. Keep in mind that your unborn baby is entirely dependent on you for nourishment. If you eat to fullness and eat healthy, nutritious food, you will gain an appropriate amount of weight for your body and your baby.

## Twins or more

'I'm expecting twins. Does this mean I should gain twice the amount of weight?'

No, don't worry, this does not mean that you should be eating for three!

It is not easy to gain the required amount of weight when you have two or more babies to worry about, but gain you must. Most doctors advise gaining about 16 to 20 kg if you are expecting twins, and around 23 kg if you are expecting triplets (a little less if you're overweight; a little more if you're underweight).

In the first trimester, when you are constantly queasy, eating smaller portions of comforting and nutritious food through the day can help you overcome the nausea. You should try to gain half kg a week in the first trimester, but if this is difficult, just be sure to take your prenatal vitamin and stay hydrated.

Your second trimester is your chance to stack up on all the nutrition your babies need to grow. Your doctor may advise half to 1 kg a week for twins; 1 to 1.25 kg a week for triplets. Supercharge your 'Square Meal' with extra servings of protein, calcium and wholegrains. If you suffer from heartburn or indigestion, eat small meals but eat frequently – spread your nutrition over 6 to 8 meals a day.

As you head into the home stretch – the third trimester – you should gain half to 1 kg per week during your seventh month. By week 32 your babies may be 2 kg each, which won't leave much room in your crowded stomach. Nevertheless, your babies still have some growing to do, so continue with your nutritious and well-balanced diet. You can expect to taper down to gaining half kg per week or less in the eighth month, and just half kg in total in the ninth.

'I'm expecting triplets... I get so tired from carrying all that bulk around, I can't wait to unload!'

Here's the good news: most multiple pregnancies don't make it to full term. On average, most multiple pregnancies last between 35 to 37 weeks. So get the weight off your feet whenever you can, and know that your ordeal will soon be over.

# FOOD

One should eat to live, not live to eat.

– Cicero

# Healthy Eating for a Healthy Pregnancy

You should eat a healthy, well-balanced diet all through life, even more so now that you have a tiny being growing inside you. Your body needs the right fuel not only to function efficiently but also to cope with the demands of your growing baby. When you consume a nutritious and balanced diet your unborn child gets well-nourished too.

Innumerable studies have shown that there is a direct correlation between a baby's health at birth and the mother's diet during pregnancy. What an expectant mother eats or doesn't eat can affect her developing foetus. Your eating habits can also have an effect on the nature of your pregnancy, your physical comfort, your emotional well-being, your labour and delivery, and even your post-partum recovery.

Here is an overview of the guidelines you should follow for nine months of stocking up on all that wholesome goodness.

## First trimester: against all odds!

In these first three months you will probably be concerned about nausea and vomiting, the dreaded 'morning sickness'. Morning sickness, unlike its name, can occur at any or all times of the day.

'I can't keep any food down because I'm throwing up all the time. Am I starving my baby?'

If you are worried about not being able to retain any of the nourishment for your baby because of vomiting, don't be anxious. Your baby will get the nourishment she needs from your reserves.

### Fit tips

⇒ Try to eat small, frequent meals, 6 to 8 times a day.
⇒ Drink plenty of liquids.
⇒ Keep busy, so you have less time to worry about throwing up.
⇒ Find ways to relax. Listen to soothing music, practise deep breathing, meditation or yoga, all of which will help calm the mind and reduce stress.

## Second trimester: smooth sailing!

This is a happier time. You stop being 'sick' and actually start enjoying being pregnant. This is a time of pleasant changes for you as your baby is developing quite rapidly. You experience the first signs of life in your tummy – your baby can now move, kick and even hear your voice. You notice your appetite getting better as your morning sickness begins to disappear.

'I crave pickle and ice-cream and can't seem to get enough of them. Is this normal during pregnancy?'

This is when your cravings kick in. Indulge in them. Enjoy the foods you crave but eat them in moderation. You need to increase your energy and protein levels by eating a well-balanced and nutritious diet.

But along with the highs come the lows. In this trimester, you may face digestive discomforts like diarrhoea or constipation, which are normal during pregnancy. As your pregnancy progresses, your digestion and elimination system get sluggish, causing bloating, gas, constipation or indigestion. It is also possible that you may become intolerant to certain foods, such as milk, paneer, cheese. Try different options that are easier to digest, such as yoghurt and buttermilk.

**Fit tips**

⇒ Continue to eat small, frequent meals and snacks.
⇒ Drink plenty of fluids.
⇒ Avoid lying down immediately after eating. Go for a short stroll instead.
⇒ Increase your caloric intake by 300 calories a day, add more protein to your diet such as pulses, soya, yoghurt, buttermilk, paneer, milk or lean meat.

## Third trimester: the home stretch

'I've grown so big... I feel stuffed and uncomfortable all the time.'

In the final three months, the growth of your baby pushes your stomach outward as the weight of your baby increases threefold. So you feel full quicker than you did earlier. It is imperative, however, to continue eating a well-balanced diet even during this trimester.

I suggest that favourite pastime – snacking! Avoid feeling stuffed by eating smaller portions more frequently. Concentrate on nutritious foods that are lighter to digest so that you are less uncomfortable. Remember, during this final trimester, your diet should provide adequate nutrition to your body, in preparation for the additional energy requirements of delivery and lactation after the baby is born.

**Fit tips**

⇒ Eat whenever you like.

⇒ Choose nutritious food. Fruits, vegetables, legumes, high fibre cereals, dairy products and fluids are essential. When you don't feel up to eating solid food you may consume soups, fruit smoothies or buttermilk.

⇒ Include garlic, fenugreek, milk and almonds in your daily diet. For instance, you can prepare garlic chutney, badam kheer or methi vegetables. These are galactogogue foods, and stimulate the production of breast milk.

# Conscious Eating

'One of the nicest things about life is the way we must regularly stop
whatever it is we are doing and devote our attention to eating.'

– Luciano Pavarotti, *Pavarotti, My Own Story*

Ayurveda tells us that the wisdom of nature is available in every
cell of our body and if we read the signals our body sends us,
we will naturally consume a healthy and balanced diet. Our
senses of sight, smell and taste are created to naturally lead us to
foods that are nourishing and beneficial; they also deter us from
consuming foods that are potentially harmful.

Thus, paying attention to the variety of flavours, aromas and
colours in the food you eat will ensure that you are getting the
diet you need in order to create a healthy body not just for you
but also for your unborn child.

Deepak Chopra, a renowned authority in the field of mind–body healing, expounds the theory of 'Eating with Awareness':

> The process of creating a body from food is miraculous. You digest, absorb and metabolise the energy and information of your food into the intelligence of your body. Simultaneously, your unborn baby extracts and metabolises the nutritional information in your blood stream into his developing body.

He explains that, from a mind–body perspective, nutrition is not limited to the food we consume. The environment in which we dine, our emotional state, even the conversations we engage in at mealtimes affect the way we digest food. How we eat is just as important as what we eat.

Try this simple exercise to experience eating with awareness. I have used this experiment with many of my clients, with great results. Arrange three different kinds of food into separate piles, say apple slices, a few almonds and some crackers. Sit down and close your eyes. Breathe in and out and allow your body to relax. Then open your eyes and choose from one of the piles. Use your senses to fully appreciate the colour, texture and aroma of the food before closing your eyes once more and taking a bite. Now use your tongue to roll it around in your mouth and analyse its flavour and feel. How do you like the taste? Does it trigger any memories? Savour each bite, chewing slowly and thoroughly before swallowing. Once you are finished with the bite, pause for a few moments and reflect on what you've noticed. My experience is that the flavours and textures will appear more vibrant to you. Repeat the process with another type of food. Note the differences or similarities in taste, aroma and the memories evoked by each.

For most of us, mealtimes are busy, noisy affairs spent catching up on the day's events with family, reading or watching television. Forget appreciating the sight and smell of food, we don't even listen when our stomach indicates that it is full, and continue to eat. Eating is a delightful experience and deserves full attention. Practise eating with awareness and silence for at least one meal a day. Devote your complete attention to savouring the flavours that nurture you.

You will notice how every bite nourishes your body and mind, leaving you free to dream of happier things!

Here are some suggestions to help increase your enjoyment at each meal:

- ✓ Eat your meals in a calm environment.
- ✓ Savour the meal.
- ✓ Avoid eating mindlessly. Stop eating when you feel satisfied.
- ✓ Do not eat when you are angry, disturbed or upset.
- ✓ Eat 6 to 8 small meals a day.
- ✓ Sit in silence for a while after finishing your meal.

**My final word**

Eating can be a spiritual and fulfilling experience. Be conscious of the food you eat at all times – whether it's a proper meal or just a snack. Remember, every bite you take is nourishment not just for you but for your baby as well. Treasure the experience.

## Food safety

'I keep reading about the chemicals, artificial colouring and preservatives found in food. Is it safe to eat these foods during pregnancy?'

This is something that almost every expectant mother worries about. Yes, the information out there is alarming and more and more is being discovered every day. Foods that were once our daily bread are being dissected and analysed and, in many cases, found wanting. But this doesn't mean you should starve yourself during pregnancy for fear of harming your baby.

Don't fret over what you cannot control, instead, try to reduce the risk whenever you can, which is not that hard with the variety of food items available these days. Take proper care in the storing and preparation of all the food you buy and you'll eat safe and ward off any food-borne diseases.

I'm not going to try and re-invent the wheel, I'm just going to remind you of these age-old principles of healthy eating.

## Shop smart

*Label check.* Check the labels of all packaged foods carefully for ingredients, nutritional information and expiry dates.

*Go organic.* Choose foods from the health food store or health section because they are usually wholesome and the ingredients carefully selected. You can opt for organic vegetables and fruits, which are rich in vitamins and minerals, without the harmful effects of pesticides.

*Fresh is best.* For optimum nutrition and safety, cook using fresh ingredients.

*Think natural.* Choose foods without colouring or artificial flavouring which are commonly found in cakes, sweets, breads, jams and savouries.

*Check the tin.* Examine cans and jars carefully for leaks, rust or damage before buying them. Check packaging labels for use-by/ expiry dates.

*Cold storage.* Ensure that the fish, meat and poultry you purchase are well-refrigerated. Put them in the freezer as soon as you get home, since changes in temperature can breed bacteria.

*Careful storage.* All raw meat, poultry and seafood should be double-wrapped and stored in a separate area of your refrigerator to maintain proper hygiene. Wipe up any spills immediately to prevent growth of bacteria.

*Take no chances.* If you think something might be spoiled because it has lost its colour or smells fishy, throw it out! Don't take the risk.

*Clean hands.* Wash your hands with warm, soapy water before handling food. Also, use a clean set of utensils and serving dishes to serve food.

*Wash your veggies.* Fruits and vegetables should be rinsed thoroughly. Even pre-cut and packaged veggies should be washed before eating.

*Cooking meat.* While cooking meat and poultry, make sure it has been well-cooked so as to destroy any bacteria.

*Keep it clean.* Kitchen counters and sinks should be cleaned regularly. All kitchen paraphernalia like spoons, forks and utensils should be washed thoroughly and frequently.

*Leftovers.* Seal leftovers in airtight containers and refrigerate immediately. Avoid consuming perishable food that has been left out for long as it may spoil.

*Eating out.* When eating out, choose restaurants that you know maintain a high standard of quality, cleanliness and hygiene.

Remember, God is in the details. Read, check, examine, and then buy. And above all, cook with care and get all the nourishment you need.

# A Square Meal

We have often heard someone say, 'He looks like he could do with a square meal.' The term 'square meal' is a slang that originated in America in the 1800s. It refers to a substantial meal that is filling and satisfying, but not necessarily healthy.

Here is my version of a ' Square Meal'. I am going to illustrate how to create the perfectly balanced meal using the analogy of a square.

Picture a square. Just as a square has four sides, your meal must have four parts to it. Each side represents an important food group – cereal, protein-rich food, fruits and vegetables and, in small quantities, fats and sugar. You need these essential food groups in the right proportions to have a balanced and healthy diet.

A balanced diet will aid you to have an easier pregnancy that is free of complications like heartburn and digestive disorders such as constipation, diarrhoea and flatulence.

To help you understand the value of a balanced diet, perform this simple experiment. Look in the mirror for telltale signs like baggy eyes, broken nails, pale skin or falling hair. What these are telling you is that your diet may be deficient in one or more of these four nutritional components. So don't wait for the signs – with a little bit of care you can give your body all the nutrition it needs, especially in these nine months.

**Health tip**

In the course of your day, I recommend three square meals – breakfast, lunch and dinner – plus 3 to 5 small snacks.

'I can't stand dal! I prefer to eat my chapatis with vegetables.'

Sorry to disappoint you, but your meal is missing its protein component. You don't have to eat dal if you dislike it; include yoghurt or drink buttermilk with your meal instead. You could also have sprouts salad, hummus or tofu, all good sources of protein.

'I prefer to eat chicken or fish with bread or rice, and tend to avoid vegetables. Is that okay?'

Vegetables contain vital vitamins and minerals essential for you and your baby during pregnancy. Eat your vegetables steamed, or ask for a side order of salad. You could also opt for vegetable soup or carrot juice for a well-balanced meal.

## How do I balance my meals?

In case you're wondering how to balance your square meals to make a wholesome pregnancy diet, I am breaking down the four major food groups to help you evaluate your three main meals and check if you are missing any vital nutrients.

### 1. Cereals

Cereals contain carbohydrates, an invaluable source of energy for the body and brain. These are an essential component of the diet and meet the increased energy demands of mother and baby. The recommended carbohydrate requirement during pregnancy is 135 to 175 grams per day to maintain the necessary blood sugar levels. Hence this food group constitutes the bulk of your requirement. Unrefined cereals, such as whole wheat bread, are better than white bread, since they retain valuable fibre and nutrients in your diet. Also in this category are grains like rice, wheat, barley, bajra, millet, jowar and oats.

## 2. Protein-rich foods

We know that proteins are the building blocks for growth. According to the Indian Council for Medical Research (ICMR), the protein requirement for a pregnant woman is 65 grams a day.

Protein is essential for:

✓ The growth of the foetus
✓ The enlargement of the uterus and development of breast tissue
✓ Increasing the mother's circulating blood volume as per the increased demand
✓ Creating reserves that will be required for labour, delivery and lactation

Complete protein is found in dairy (skimmed or whole), eggs and meat. You can increase your intake of milk or yoghurt for your increased calcium and protein requirements. If milk and milk products have become difficult to tolerate, consume yoghurt or buttermilk instead.

**Non-vegetarians** should consume meat that is lean, such as chicken, fish and meat. You can consume up to three eggs a week to receive the health benefits you need. Remember, egg yolks are higher in cholesterol than egg whites. Avoid eating raw egg as it may lead to bacterial infections. Instead, eat your eggs boiled, poached or scrambled.

If you are **vegetarian**, it is much easier and safer to follow a lacto-ovo diet (a diet that includes milk and eggs) during pregnancy. Consume adequate quantities of milk and milk products, pulses, sprouts, nuts, seeds and soya products.

In a **vegan diet**, it is important to eat the right food in the right combinations and proportions. For example, combining incomplete protein sources such as legumes (dal or beans) or nuts with grains provides the body with complete protein.

> **Fit fact:** Soya milk and soya products are excellent sources of protein. Soya is the only plant food that contains all nine essential amino acids in sufficient proportions to be considered a complete protein.

### 3. Fruits and vegetables

This is a vital food group for your vitamin and mineral requirements. Fruits and vegetables contain fibre, which assists bowel movements. Diets low in fibre often result in constipation, a common concern during pregnancy. The requirement of fibre during pregnancy is 28 grams a day.

Think about colour when you eat – different coloured fruits and vegetables have different nutritional properties. Mix and match various colours to give you a range of vitamins and minerals. Try to eat your veggies lightly cooked, since overcooking can destroy their natural nutrients. For additional benefit, opt for seasonal fruits and vegetables. Citrus fruits such as oranges, sweet lime and watermelon will keep you cool; for more filling options try bananas, mangoes, chikoo and custard apples. And if you've got a sweet tooth, have dried fruits like dates, prunes, figs, raisins and apricots.

### 4. Sugar and fat

Your sugar requirement can be obtained naturally, in the form of fructose, from fruit. Additional sugar in the form of mithai and cakes should be limited.

The body needs fat to build cells, provide energy, conserve body heat and protect the organs from damage. Fat also helps in the absorption of vitamins A, D, E and K. Examples of fat are butter, ghee, cream and oil. Consume fats and sugar in small quantities (5 to 6 teaspoons a day) to avoid excess weight gain.

Essential fatty acids are also required for the normal development of the foetal nervous system and immune system. Your baby extracts the required fats from your circulation, so you must include them in your diet. The two main categories of essential fats are omega-3 and omega-6 fatty acids. Omega-6 fatty acids are found in most seed- and nut-derived oils such as almond, corn, safflower, sesame, sunflower and walnut. Seed oils contain relatively low levels of omega-3 fatty acids, with the exception of flaxseed, canola and soybean.

How to add omega-3 to your diet:

✓   Cook with canola or soybean oil.
✓   Garnish salads and sautéed vegetables with roasted flaxseed.
✓   Eat 2 to 3 walnuts every day.
✓   Consume well-cooked fish. Avoid large fish like king mackerel as it contains high levels of mercury.
✓   Toss your salad in olive oil dressing.

---

**Recommended dietary allowance***
(*as recommended by the ICMR)
Indian women with a moderate activity level need an additional 300 calories a day during pregnancy. This is required for:
✓   Growth of the foetus and placenta
✓   Increased energy requirements of the mother in carrying the weight of the foetus

To get you started on your Square Meal plan, here is a sample daily menu:

## On waking up
- Weak tea
- Dry crackers (if nauseous)

## Breakfast (one of the following)
- Muesli or porridge with a few raisins and 5 almonds and milk
- 1 to 2 slices of multigrain toast, fresh fruit with yoghurt and nuts
- Idli-sambar/poha/upma/wholegrain toast; fresh fruit and a glass of milk
- Multigrain toast, omelette, fruit

## Mid-morning (2 to 3 hours after breakfast)
- Fruit juice or a glass of milk

## Lunch
- 1 bowl salad with cucumber, tomatoes, carrots, lettuce and sprouts
- 2 to 3 chapatis (wheat, jowar, soya, bajra) or 1 cup rice
- 1 bowl cooked vegetables
- 1 cup dal (preferably mung dal) or 1 piece chicken/fish
- A glass of buttermilk

## Tea
- 1 cup tea/milk with multigrain crackers
- 1 bowl mixed fruit

## Dinner
- 1 bowl salad
- 2 to 3 chapatis or 1 cup rice

☞ 1 bowl cooked vegetables
☞ 1 cup dal or 1 piece chicken/fish
☞ 1 cup yoghurt or a glass of buttermilk

**Bedtime** (if required)
☞ A glass of warm milk

*Note:* This is a sample diet plan. If you have any weight concerns (in case you are overweight or underweight) please consult your gynaecologist for specific dietary recommendations.

'I'm a fast food junkie! I need my cheesy pizza, frankie and channa bhatura at least five times a week. I know it's not good for me during pregnancy but what can I do?'

This is a pet peeve among many of my clients. If you can't live without fast food, don't be alarmed – you don't have to. Just make smart choices so that you don't end up piling on too many kilos. Listed below are some ways to help you 'have your cake and eat it too':

How to convert fast food into a Square Meal

✓ Pizza: wholewheat base with extra veggies, low on cheese
✓ Frankie: roti roll with veggies and chicken tikka/paneer
✓ Pasta: wholewheat pasta with veggies, paneer or chicken (with any light tomato-based sauce, avoid creamy, cheesy sauces)
✓ Channa bhatura: channa and tandoori roti with fresh veggie salad
✓ Burger: wholegrain burger with meat/veggie patty and coleslaw
✓ Medu vada or idli-sambar: ask for extra veggies
✓ Noodles: wholewheat noodles with veggies and chicken/tofu/paneer

## Good calories vs bad calories

### Weighing the pros and cons

First of all, what is a calorie? In layman's terms, a calorie is a measure of the food energy we consume, which is burned or stored by the body as fat. So when you hear about 'good' and 'bad calorie' foods, what does it mean?

At a very basic level, let me tell you that there is no such thing as 'bad food'. However, certain foods, such as cookies and fast food like French fries and burgers, contribute more calories than nutrients. Food manufacturers process the raw ingredients, often adding trans fats to enhance taste and prolong the shelf life of the product. A high intake of trans fat can raise low-density cholesterol levels and increase the risk of cardiovascular disease. Therefore, if consumed in excess, these food products are considered 'bad' or 'harmful'.

Just imagine, a large burger with fries and a cola contains more than half your total daily calorie recommendation! An occasional burger is fine, if you keep it as an occasional treat only.

'What do excess calories do? They just get into your wardrobe at night and sew your clothes tighter.'

While it is true that excess calorie consumption could make your clothes tighter, you should be aware that 'all calories are not equal'. You might gain the same number of calories from a slice of cake or a deep-fried snack as from a wholegrain muffin or a baked snack, but the former will do you more harm than good. So choose your calories with care and opt for quality over quantity, especially when you're pregnant. Your baby and your body will thank you for it.

Healthy snacking gives you a huge energy boost in the long run, unlike the temporary high from processed or refined food.

Find alternatives that can replace your favourite munchies and still keep you happy.

My rule of thumb: go natural. While the calorie counts of these foods remain the same, brown bread is healthier than white and brown rice is better than white. Natural or wholegrain food products are healthier because they are high in fibre and take longer to digest. The glucose in these unprocessed foods is released more gradually into your bloodstream. On the other hand, with processed food, the energy boost lasts only for a short while, after which your energy levels come crashing down, resulting in mood swings.

The bottom line: a wholewheat or multigrain sandwich with a filling of your choice is always a healthier, more satisfying option than its white counterpart.

> **Fit tip:** Some manufacturers add food colour to regular white bread, to make it 'brown' and pass it off as a high-fibre product. Check for words like 'wholewheat', 'multigrain' or 'wholegrain' on labels for bread, biscuits, pastas and other baked products.

## Sweet tooth!

'Sugar and spice and all things nice... that's what little girls are made of.'

We have all grown up listening to this rhyme but the truth is that today we are discovering that sugar is not all that 'nice'. Researchers have found that sugar, in excessive amounts, is potentially harmful. Not only does it lead to obesity, too much sugar may also contribute to tooth decay, diabetes, heart disease and colon cancer.

'I love desserts! I must have some chocolate, mithai or ice-cream after my meal. Am I harming my baby?'

If you must have sweets for that all important 'pick-me-up', go ahead! But set yourself a limit – eat a few pieces of chocolate instead of a whole bar. You could also try to substitute dessert with more nutritious options like fruit, dried fruit and fruit juice concentrates. These contain vitamins, trace minerals and phytochemicals (plant chemicals that help fight disease and aging), none of which is found in sugar.

And if this doesn't satisfy your sweet tooth, cut back on portion size. Eat smaller portions and share dessert – remember, half a portion is better than none at all!

## Food supplements

Getting the right nutrition is always important but right now it's more important than ever. Just to make doubly sure that you are consuming all the essential nutrients vital to your baby's growth and development, doctors often ask you to take supplements.

### Prenatal supplements and vitamins

'Why do I need prenatal supplements or vitamins if I eat all the right foods?'

Many of my clients who follow my Square Meal diet ask me why they need to take pills to supplement the nutritive value of what they eat, when they are so careful about eating the 'right' food. Let me tell you what I tell them – we cannot measure the exact value of everything we eat, so a prenatal supplement will give you that extra health insurance for you and your baby.

But keep in mind that a supplement is merely meant to supplement your meal – not replace it! The best way to get your daily dose of vitamins and minerals is from natural food sources, because fresh food not only contains the essential nutrients but also the wholesome goodness that nature has to offer.

**Remember:** Always consult your doctor before taking any supplements.

## Iron

Iron helps manufacture an adequate supply of haemoglobin, which is important for you when you're pregnant, since you experience a 40 to 50 per cent increase in blood volume during this time. Your unborn baby is also storing iron which she will need for the first few months of her life outside your womb. The baby takes what is required from your store of iron first, so it won't suffer if your intake is inadequate. However, you will end up with anaemia, a haemoglobin deficiency that can make you tired and makes it harder for your blood to carry oxygen through your body and to the baby. Iron is also required for the proper development of the cells and organs in your baby's body and for the growth of the placenta, especially in the second and third trimesters.

These foods are rich in iron:
- Enriched grains
- Dried beans and peas
- Dried fruits
- Dark leafy green vegetables like spinach and broccoli
- Blackstrap molasses such as raisins, figs
- Iron-fortified breakfast cereals
- Red meat and poultry

**Recommended dosage:** 38 mg a day for pregnant women.

So pregnant women have the greatest need for iron supplementation. A pregnant woman's iron requirement is almost double that of a non-pregnant woman, due to potential blood loss during delivery and increased blood volume during gestation. Iron deficiency during pregnancy is also associated with pre-term labour, low birth weight and infant mortality.

**Fit tip:** Take your iron supplement with a glass of orange juice, since the vitamin C in the juice will aid the absorption of iron. Avoid taking iron with milk, because calcium blocks absorption.

## Folic acid

Another critical nutrient in pregnancy is folic acid (vitamin B9 or folate, as it is known in its natural state).

Folic acid helps prevent neural tube defects which are serious birth defects of the spinal cord and the brain. Neural tube defects can occur at a very early stage of development, before many women even know they're pregnant. Studies have shown that taking folic acid one month prior to and during the first three months of pregnancy decreases the risk of neural tube defects by up to 70 per cent. Vitamin B is critical to the rapid growth of the placenta and your developing baby.

The neural tube, formed in the early weeks of pregnancy, goes on to become the baby's developing brain and spinal cord. When the neural tube does not form properly, the result is a neural tube defect.

These foods are rich in folic acid:
- Almonds and peanuts
- Wheat germ
- Leafy green vegetables, bottle gourd (lauki), pumpkin
- Legumes
- Soya
- Citrus fruits

**Recommended dosage:** Pregnant women should take 400 to 800 mg folic acid per day during pregnancy.

## Calcium

When you're pregnant, your developing baby needs calcium to build strong bones and teeth and to develop normal heart rhythm and blood-clotting abilities. Thus it is essential to increase your calcium intake to protect your calcium resources and to meet the increased demand during lactation. Loss of calcium from your bones may impair your own health later on.

These foods are rich in calcium
- Low-fat dairy products: milk, cottage cheese, pasteurised cheese and yoghurt
- Calcium fortified products: orange juice, soya milk and cereals
- Dark green vegetables: spinach, kale and broccoli
- Tofu
- Dried beans
- Almonds

**Recommended dosage:** Pregnant women should take 1,000 mg per day.

**Fit tip:** Continue to take calcium even after you have finished nursing, since you will need the mineral to help strengthen bones and ward off bone loss (osteoporosis) later in life.

## Vitamin D

Vitamin D helps the body absorb calcium and may help prevent osteoporosis later in life. Latest research suggests that vitamin D is required for enhanced immune function and brain development in your foetus. Vitamin D deficiency can lead to your baby being born with delayed bone ossification and defective enamel formation in the teeth.

These are rich in vitamin D:
- Dairy products
- Fish
- Egg yolk
- Sunlight

**Recommended dosage:** Pregnant women should take at least 5 mcg per day, for calcium absorption and healthy bones.

**Fit tip:** For the required dose of vitamin D, try to get 10 to 15 minutes of early morning sunlight on your arms, legs and face, at least thrice a week.

## Zinc

The mineral zinc is essential for the development of the embryo. Zinc is necessary for cell division, and growth and for improving immune function, digestion and metabolism. It plays an important role in the health of the reproductive organs, it is needed to maintain vitamin E levels in the blood, and aids in the absorption of vitamin A. Zinc deficiency in pregnant women can cause loss of appetite and reduced resistance to infection.

These foods are rich in zinc:
- Meat
- Seafood
- Poultry
- Milk
- Eggs
- Mushrooms
- Soya beans
- Sunflower and pumpkin seeds
- Wheat germ

**Recommended dosage:** Pregnant women need 11 to 13 mg per day.

## Essential fatty acids

Long chain fatty acids, also known as omega-3 and omega-6 fatty acids, are important for foetal growth and development. Specifically, a type of omega-3 fatty acid known as DHA, which aids brain and retina development, can lead to a significant reduction in the incidence of premature delivery.

> These foods are rich in fatty acids:
> - Fish oil
> - Walnuts
> - Flax seeds
>
> **Recommended dosage:** 300 mg to 400 mg of a DHA rich omega-3 fatty acid.

## Vitamin B12

This vitamin is essential for proper nerve and brain function in both mother and baby. Do you know that the foetus requires twice the amount of vitamin B12 as compared to the mother? Low levels are associated with premature delivery. The capacity of a woman to absorb B12 increases during pregnancy as a large amount is required by the foetus. A word of caution: vegetarian mothers are more likely to become B12 deficient.

> These foods are rich in vitamin B12:
> - Animal products: animal liver and poultry
> - Fortified soya milk
> - Bean sprouts (mung, chawli, vaal)
> - Kidney beans (rajma)
> - Bengal gram and black gram
>
> **Recommended dosage:** A normal adult woman's requirement of vitamin B12 is 1 mcg and this requirement remains the same during pregnancy.

## Vitamin C

Vitamin C is required for building immunity. The foetal requirement for this vitamin is small and supplementation may not be necessary during pregnancy.

Low intake of vitamin C is associated with premature rupture of the foetal membrane.

These foods are rich in vitamin C:
- Grapefruit
- Oranges
- Strawberries
- Tomatoes
- Vegetables: raw cabbage, green pepper, broccoli, cauliflower and raw spinach

**Recommended dosage:** The Indian Council of Medical Research recommendations of vitamin C during pregnancy are 40 mg – the same as when you are not pregnant.

## Protein

Protein is required for growth and development. It is the building block of all tissues. Protein intake should be increased by 10 to 15 grams a day; it can easily be found in animal products, including meats, milk and eggs. Some plant food, such as dal, sprouts and cereal grains can also provide high quality protein.

These foods are rich in protein:
- Dal
- Soya bean
- Lentils
- Sprouts
- Eggs ( especially egg white)
- Fish
- Meat or chicken

# Kitchen Comfort
## A Guide to Shopping and Stocking during Pregnancy

A cook is only as good as her pantry. Have you seen cooking shows on TV where the hostess reaches into her pantry to get whatever she wants – and it is always right there! Haven't you stared enviously and longingly at their pantry and wished it were yours? I know I have!

Take Nigella Lawson, chef, TV host and author extraordinaire; her pantry makes me so envious. She has food from all over the world in there. In her own words, she is whimsical and plans for a rainy day by stocking everything under the sun... she never knows what she will fancy eating!

'I never really appreciated the practicality of stocking until I was pregnant. I used to be hungry all the time and would end up munching on anything I could find – chips, chiwda, chocolate. It was only later that I realized that the key to eating healthy foods was to have them accessible. So I started stocking healthy savouries such as khakra, roasted kurmura (puffed rice), popcorn and wholewheat crackers. I reserved a couple of shelves in the kitchen for myself so that I knew exactly where to find my snack whenever I got the munchies... Life became so much simpler!'

My client Shalini Iyer learnt to adopt a common sense approach to life. She started stocking healthy, nutritious snacks in her kitchen. Her philosophy – she couldn't eat what she didn't have. So make sure you stock the food you need, especially for that rainy day!

'I often find myself in the supermarket, clutching the trolley, staring at racks and racks of foodstuff. I didn't even know there are so many varieties of fruits and vegetables. It's overwhelming... What do I buy?'

Shopping for food is an art. I am going to help you figure out how and what to stock and you will master it in no time. Think variety, especially now that you are pregnant! Different fruits and vegetables are rich in different vitamins, minerals and fibre. So aim for variety and pick them across the rainbow spectrum.

*Green leafy vegetables:* Green leafy vegetables such as spinach, lettuce and other greens are rich in iron, beta-carotene, chlorophyll and dietary fibre. The darker the coloured greens, the more nutritious and higher the beta-carotene content.

*Fruit vegetables:* 'Fruit' vegetables such as tomatoes, squash and peppers contain ripened seeds of pollinated flowers. These are filling, yet low in calories.

*Flowers, buds and stalks:* Flowers, buds and stalks include celery, cauliflower, broccoli and asparagus. These plants are rich in dietary fibre and vitamin C.

*Roots and bulbs:* Roots and bulbs are the parts of a plant that store nutrients. Vegetables such as beet, onions and carrots are mineral-rich and filling.

*Seeds and pods:* Examples are peas, green beans, okra and drumstick. These vegetables contain more protein than other vegetables do.

Remember, fresh, wholesome food never goes out of fashion. You will recall your mother cooking it when you were a child. What was good for you then will be good for you and for your baby too. Once your kitchen is well-stocked with all the wholesome goodness that you and your unborn child need, you will settle into the right eating plan.

Get creative, make your own recipes and menus. Experiment with different cuisines and introduce new tastes and flavours to your diet.

Become the Nigella of your own home. Take it from me and other food gurus – a good healthy diet not only results in a smoother pregnancy but lowers the risk of many diseases, including the onset of diabetes and cancer. Remember, healthy eating begins at home. The next time you go to the supermarket, go armed with my healthy shopping list.

# Cut and keep this list for easy reference to help you plan your daily requirements. Tick any item you might need.

**Fruit**
- ☐ Melon
- ☐ Apples
- ☐ Pomegranate
- ☐ Pears
- ☐ Figs
- ☐ Strawberries
- ☐ Pineapple
- ☐ Orange/Sweet lime
- ☐ Any other

**Vegetables**
- ☐ Tomatoes
- ☐ Lettuce
- ☐ Cabbage
- ☐ Spinach
- ☐ Carrots
- ☐ Pumpkin
- ☐ Okra
- ☐ Potatoes
- ☐ Cucumber
- ☐ Broccoli
- ☐ Cauliflower
- ☐ Aubergine
- ☐ Onions
- ☐ Any other

**Breads**
- ☐ Wholegrain
- ☐ Rye
- ☐ Multigrain

**Cereals**
- ☐ Rice (preferably unpolished/brown)
- ☐ Oats/raagi/broken wheat
- ☐ Chapati (jowar/bajra/soya/nachni/wheat)
- ☐ Pasta (wheat)
- ☐ Wholegrain crackers
- ☐ Roasted savouries (popcorn, puffed rice, poha, khakra)
- ☐ Ready-to-eat breakfast cereals (muesli, oat flakes, wheat flakes, rice flakes)

**Oils/Lentils/Herbs/Condiments**
- ☐ Oils such as olive oil, peanut oil, sunflower oil, canola oil
- ☐ Honey
- ☐ Spices (chaat masala/mustard/seasonings)
- ☐ Dal (mung dal is the lightest of dals and is easy to digest)
- ☐ Sprouted mung/alfalfa/chickpeas
- ☐ Cinnamon
- ☐ Nutmeg
- ☐ Turmeric
- ☐ Basil/oregano/rosemary/dill/parsley
- ☐ Fresh green coriander
- ☐ Fresh mint leaves

**Dairy**
- ☐ Milk
- ☐ Soya milk
- ☐ Cottage cheese
- ☐ Yoghurt
- ☐ Feta cheese

**Nuts/Seeds**
- ☐ Almond/cashew/pecan/walnut
- ☐ Sesame/pumpkin/sunflower/watermelon seeds
- ☐ Chikki (made of seeds, nuts and jaggery)

**Meat/Fish/Eggs**
- ☐ Chicken
- ☐ Fish
- ☐ Eggs (consume egg whites, limit egg yolks to 2 to 3 per week)

**Beverages**
- ☐ Coconut water
- ☐ Herbal tea
- ☐ Coffee/tea
- ☐ Bottled water (if required)
- ☐ Fresh juice

**Any other**
- ☐
- ☐
- ☐

# Snack Time
## Healthy Snacking between Meals

'Keep your worries at bay, as you snack on food all day.
For a very pregnant you, this is exactly what you should do.'

– Tarla Dalal

Set aside all the diet books that tell you not to snack between meals. You are pregnant now and have two mouths to feed! Remember, your foetus needs regular nourishment at regular intervals.

The rule of thumb during pregnancy is 6 to 8 meals a day, which means you should be snacking at least 3 to 5 times a day. So make the most of this invaluable opportunity to stock up on all the healthy nutrients your growing baby needs.

You now have a licence to snack through the day, but think before you reach out for a bag of chips or that tempting plate of chaat or samosa – you need to fulfil your snack cravings in a healthy way.

Smart snacking is a choice you have to make. Here are some tips to help you enjoy your snacks and avoid piling on too many extra calories:

✓ Include more fruits and vegetables to add fibre to your diet.
✓ Avoid deep-fried and oily foods such as wafers, cheese balls and chivda and substitute with baked or roasted snacks such as popcorn, khakra, kurmura. Select snacks that are nutritionally healthy.
✓ Avoid aerated drinks – these contain empty calories and have no nutritive value. They only help you put on weight.
✓ Read the labels very carefully. Select foods with minimum fat, sugar and salt. If you snack out, choose the snack carefully and eat well-heated products.

## High in energy

My client Meena, three months pregnant, asked me a question that is probably worrying many of you. 'I feel ravenous throughout the day and get quite exhausted by the evening. Is there any food I can eat to keep my energy levels up?' Here are some options that are a great pick-me-up whenever you need a boost of energy:

### Banana: a high-energy fruit to fill you up

Bananas are good for the nerves and muscles, and enhance the functioning of the immune system. Rich in potassium and sugar, they provide the body with nourishment and instant energy. A large banana has about 100 calories. It is richer in solids and lower in water content than most fresh fruit and provides quick recovery from fatigue.

**Tip:** Blend bananas with milk, water and honey for a delicious smoothie.

### Sprouts: an energy-enhancing food

Filling and low in calories, sprouts are high in valuable amino acid (protein) content. Popular sprouts are mung, alfalfa, kidney beans and chickpeas.

**Tip:** Add sprouts to sandwiches and salads.

### Yoghurt: cooling and filling

Yoghurt is a delicious, filling snack that comes in an array of flavours. It contains probiotics, which are responsible for several activities in your gut, such as producing lactase and improving the functioning of your digestive tract. Yoghurt also boosts your immune system.

**Tip:** Garnish with fresh fruit and honey.

## Five snack options at restaurants

1. Multigrain sandwich with loads of vegetables
2. Tandoori dishes
3. Roti wrap
4. Greek salad
5. Dhokla/idli/dosa/uttapam with sambar

## Ten snack options at home

| | |
|---|---|
| 1. | Trail mix |
| 2. | Roasted puffed rice |
| 3. | Popcorn |
| 4. | A fistful of nuts: peanuts/cashew nuts/almonds |
| 5. | Corn on the cob |
| 6. | Banana |
| 7. | Apple with a cheese cube |
| 8. | Guava (garnished with chilli powder and salt) |
| 9. | Cucumber/carrot/celery strips (with rock salt) |
| 10. | Chutney and tomato sandwich (on wholewheat bread) |

To get you started, here are some healthy recipes for snacks:

## Dalia Upma

*Serves 4*

### Ingredients
4 cups broken wheat dalia (6 cups soaked)
1 medium onion, chopped
1 cup mixed vegetables (carrots, cauliflower, potatoes, green beans –
diced and steamed)
½ cup corn kernels
½ tsp mustard seeds
A pinch of asafoetida (*hing*)
A handful of curry leaves
½ inch ginger, grated
3 slit green chillies
A pinch of turmeric powder
2 tsp oil
2 cups water
Chopped coriander leaves to garnish
2 tbsp lime juice
Salt to taste

**Method**

Roast dalia in a pan on low flame until light brown in colour. Remove from pan and set aside.

Heat the oil in the pan, add mustard seeds, asafoetida and curry leaves. When the mustard seeds splutter, add grated ginger and slit green chillies.

Add the chopped onion and stir. Then add the diced vegetables. Stir for about 5 minutes and add the roasted dalia. Season with salt and turmeric powder.

Add 2 cups water and put into a pressure cooker for 1 or 2 whistles or until the dalia is soft and crumbly.

Squeeze lime juice over it and garnish with chopped coriander leaves. Serve hot.

## Mung Chaat

*Serves 4*

**Ingredients**

4 cups sprouted mung, with the skin (lightly steamed)
3 tomatoes, chopped
1 potato, boiled and diced
2 carrots, diced
1 bunch green onions, chopped
½ tsp lime juice
1 tsp chaat masala
½ cup fresh coriander leaves, chopped

**Method**

Steam the mung sprouts for 3 to 4 minutes, retaining the crunch. Cool the sprouts. Add all the other ingredients, mix well and serve.

## Sautéed Tofu

*Serves 4*

**Ingredients**

16 cubes low-fat tofu
2 tsp green garlic, finely chopped
1 tsp oil
Chilli flakes (optional)
½ tsp coarse ground pepper
Salt to taste

### Method

Heat the oil and sauté the garlic in a pan. Add the tofu cubes and the spices. Sauté for a few minutes. Serve hot.

## Poha with Potatoes and Peas

*Serves 4*

### Ingredients

6 cups poha (8 cups soaked)
1½ cups peas and potatoes, diced and boiled
1 large onion, chopped
½ tsp oil
¼ tsp mustard seeds
A pinch of asafoetida (hing)
A handful of curry leaves
3 slit green chillies
2 pods garlic, crushed (optional)
A pinch of turmeric
2 tsp lime juice
Chopped coriander leaves to garnish
2 cups water
Salt to taste

### Method

Wash the poha gently in running water, and soak for 3 to 4 minutes. Lightly squeeze out the water and set aside. Heat oil in a kadhai, add mustard seeds, asafoetida, curry leaves, green chillies and garlic. Stir in the onions, peas and potatoes, and cook until the onion is transparent.

Add the soaked poha, salt and turmeric. Mix all the ingredients well, and add ¼ cup water, if required. When the water dries up, sprinkle lime juice and garnish with coriander leaves. Serve hot.

## Fruit Chaat

*Serves 4*

### Ingredients

4 cups mixed fruit, chopped
1 tsp chaat masala
½ tsp lime juice

### Method

Sprinkle fruit with chaat masala and lime juice and serve.

# Mixed Peppers Omelette

*Serves 2*

### Ingredients
8 egg whites or 2 whole eggs
1 tsp milk
2 onions, finely chopped
1 red bell pepper, diced
1 yellow bell pepper, diced
1 green bell pepper, diced
1 tomato, finely chopped
Fresh coriander leaves, chopped
½ green chilli, finely chopped
3 olives, chopped (optional)
¼ tsp chilli powder
½ tsp olive oil/ghee
Salt to taste

### Method
Whip up the eggs, milk and salt. Add all the vegetables and continue beating until the mixture is light and frothy. Heat the oil. When it is hot, pour in the egg-vegetable mixture.

Cover the pan, and let the omelette cook for about 2 or 3 minutes. If you require it brown on both sides, flip over. Sprinkle with fresh pepper if desired. Serve hot on multigrain bread.

# Greek Salad with Wholewheat Croutons

*Serves 4*

This is an extremely nutritious snack because vegetables are fibre-rich, feta cheese gives you protein, and olive oil comes with heart-friendly benefits.

### Ingredients
1 bunch iceberg lettuce leaves
16 cubes low-fat feta cheese
8 pitted black olives
2 red onions, sliced
2 ripe tomatoes, diced
1 tsp balsamic vinegar

½ tsp coarsely crushed pepper
2 teaspoons olive oil
4 large slices wholewheat bread (for the croutons)
Salt to taste

### Method

In a large bowl, tear the lettuce leaves and crumble the feta. Add diced olives and onion. Drizzle balsamic vinegar, 1 tsp olive oil, and add salt and pepper to taste. Mix well.

Mix the remaining olive oil and salt in a small bowl. Spread this mixture on the bread slices, on both sides. Cut the bread slices into little squares and toast in a hot pan till they turn crisp and golden brown. When the bread croutons cool, add to the salad and serve immediately.

## Paneer Cutlet Sandwich

*Serves 4*

You could keep the paneer mixture ready in the fridge, so all you do is shape and shallow-fry the cutlets when you are hungry.

### Ingredients
8 slices multigrain bread

*For the paneer cutlet:*
3 cups crumbled paneer
1 cup potato, boiled and mashed
1 tsp cumin powder
1 tsp coriander powder
1 tsp chilli powder
2 tsp lime juice
2 green chillies, finely chopped
1 tsp oil
Salt to taste

### Method

Mix the paneer with the mashed potato, add the masalas, green chillies, lime juice and salt. Let it form a dough-like consistency. Shape the mixture into four cutlets. Heat oil in a pan, shallow-fry the cutlets till they are golden brown on both sides. Place each cutlet between two slices of bread. Serve with mint chutney.

## A guide to eating junk food during pregnancy

'I'm a real junk food junkie! I can't live without chips, samosas, chaat or malai kulfi. I know these are bad for me during pregnancy, but what do I do?'

The fact that you recognize that this kind of food is bad for you and your baby at this time is the biggest step to changing your eating habits. There's a reason it's called 'junk food' – because that's exactly what you should do with it – junk it! Make a serious effort to change your eating habits and remember: it's worth it!

Here are my suggestions to overcome your addiction to junk food:

*At the office:* Eat a wholesome breakfast at home before you leave for work. If you normally start your day at work with a cup of coffee, stop! Have green tea or fresh fruit juice instead. Feeling peckish at work? Order a healthy sandwich from the cafeteria.

*Carry your snacks:* Stock your home, office and bag with wholesome, satisfying snacks such as fresh fruit, trail mix, granola bars and crackers, kurmura, khakra, yoghurt, smoothies and plenty of bottled water. This practice will keep you from straying back to your old habits and will ensure you eat well throughout your pregnancy.

*Substitute:* Instead of your usual cream biscuit, have a bran muffin with your morning coffee or tea. Substitute your after-dinner ice-cream or dessert with a fresh fruit smoothie or fresh fruit salad. Thankfully, there is an abundance of healthy snacks available for the health conscious, so you never have to go without.

Here are my picks for healthy 'junk' food options:

✓ Khakra, low-fat bhelpuri, soya nuggets, baked mung chakli, date sweets and multigrain biscuits are tasty and healthy choices.
✓ Granola bars make a great substitute for chocolate bars.
✓ Roasted nuts (only a handful) can replace wafers or salted, deep-fried nuts.
✓ Instead of aerated beverages, drink fresh fruit juice, coconut water or good old nimbu pani.

Important fail-safe methods to adopt:

✓ Make healthier choices when eating out; don't be shy about asking questions about ingredients.
✓ Read the labels carefully to know what you are consuming.
✓ Beware of misleading terms such as 'low-fat' – they may contain extra sugar or other refined ingredients.

Remember, good habits, just like their bad counterparts, can last a lifetime. Make the effort to develop healthier eating habits for yourself and your family and you will have a happier, healthier family for life!

## Caffeine

'I need a cup of coffee first thing in the morning... I can't wake up without it! I consume at least two more cups at work. Is it true that caffeine is not safe during pregnancy?'

If you are not able to eliminate coffee consumption, drink less than 200 mg or two cups of coffee per day. According to some research, women who consume 200 mg or more caffeine a day may double their risk of miscarriage.

You should be aware that the caffeine present in coffee, tea, colas and other soft beverages crosses the placenta and enters foetal circulation, doing more harm than good. So if you are a caffeine addict, take heed, here's what can happen:

✓ Caffeine has a diuretic effect.
✓ It draws fluid and calcium from the body.
✓ Coffee and tea, especially when taken with milk or cream and sugar, tend to fill you up, spoiling your appetite for the nutritious food you need.
✓ Colas are not only filling but may contain questionable chemicals and unnecessary sugar.
✓ Caffeine can exacerbate your normal pregnancy mood swings and keep you up when you should be resting.
✓ Caffeine may interfere with the absorption of iron.

How to break the caffeine habit:

✓ Switch to a decaffeinated alternative.
✓ Substitute colas with unsweetened fruit juices.
✓ If you crave a caffeine lift, try some exercise instead, for a more natural and longer-lasting high.

Trust me, within a few days of giving up caffeine, you will begin to feel better than ever!

## Hungry kya?

Here are my ten favourite pick-me-ups when I am hungry. Feel free to add your own!

### Wholegrain wrap
Wrap and roll with a filling of your choice. Roll vegetables, spreads, paneer bhurji or spicy potato filling in a roti or pita.

### Multigrain sandwich
Lettuce and tomato, cucumber, sprouts, avocado, paneer, chicken, fish, jam – the choices are endless! Experiment with different fillings.

### Mini meal
Mini vegetable or chicken cutlets, kebabs, patties, idli and uttapam make delectable bite-size snacks.

### Wholewheat pita pocket
Seal up some hummus, drippy cheese-and-veggie or chicken filling in these tasty bites.

### Veggie hot dog
Stuff a hot dog multigrain bun with a long veggie patty.

### Idli sandwich
Steamed idlis make a great sandwich with fillings like mint chutney, tomato chutney or even cheese.

### Bhel and chaat
Make a healthy version of this lip-smacking street food. Mix crunchy mung sprouts, potato and a bit of sev with tamarind date chutney; it's a real treat for chaat lovers.

---

**Stir-fried vegetables with rice**
Really hungry? Rustle up a vegetable fried rice, a veggie pulao or even a chicken hot pot.

**Cold pasta salad**
Pasta mixed with seasonal vegetables and topped with a tomato-based sauce is an all-time favourite.

**Stuffed paratha**
Always delicious, parathas can be stuffed with a filling of your choice – grated vegetables, paneer, corn or the trusted potato – and cooked with a little ghee on the tawa.

---

## Water for two!

'Pure water is the first and foremost medicine.'

– Slovakian proverb

During pregnancy, you're not only eating for two, you are also drinking for two!

Your baby's body, like yours, is composed mostly of fluid. As your baby grows, so does its demand for fluids. Your body too needs fluids more than ever, since pregnancy pumps up fluid volume significantly. You should consume at least 8 to 12 glasses of water per day.

**'I am scared to drink water, especially at work or when I'm out, for fear of going to the loo too often.'**

Frequent urination is a by-product of pregnancy because of the additional pressure on your bladder, but the benefits of drinking adequate water outweigh the discomforts. You will feel the urge to urinate more frequently, especially in your third trimester. Relieve yourself as often as you need to so as not to burden your bladder and cause other problems like water retention.

Drink 2 to 3 litres of water every day to counter this loss of fluids. Keeping your body well-hydrated reduces the risk of urinary tract infections, kidney stones and constipation.

'I have never been a big water drinker. Sometimes I go for hours before I take a sip of water. Is this bad for me and my baby?'

It is time to change your habits. 65 to 70 per cent of your body is made up of water, which is why you need minimum eight glasses a day for your body to function properly. Lack of water can cause severe problems like dehydration, low blood pressure, constipation and poor metabolic function. Even mild dehydration can prevent the kidneys from effectively purifying the blood, which means the toxins keep building up in your system. Symptoms like nausea or drowsiness can accompany these conditions. The additional effects of drinking adequate water are soft, glowing skin, sparkling eyes and shining hair.

How do you know you are consuming enough water? The colour of your urine is a good indicator of your hydration levels. If you are drinking enough fluids your urine will be almost clear in colour. The less water you drink the darker your urine will be.

*Please note:* Certain kinds of medication may affect the colour of your urine.

## Every glass counts!

Start your day with a glass of water. You can have warm water with lemon, or drink it slightly chilled or at room temperature. Water with lemon is a great source of vitamin C and helps stimulate the bowels. Gradually teach yourself to have two glasses before breakfast. Sip the water slowly (avoid gulping), giving your body a few minutes to absorb it before breakfast.

Here are some tips to keep your water levels up:

✓ Carry a bottle of water with you everywhere you go.
✓ Keep sipping water while exercising or travelling.
✓ Get into the habit of drinking water through the day.
✓ Drink water before you are thirsty. Thirst is not felt until you are already dehydrated.
✓ Increase your intake of fresh fruits and vegetables, as they have high water content.

# Fine Dining
## Eating Out Pregnancy Style

Pregnant woman: 'I'll have two of each! I'm eating for two!'
Man: 'I'll have a bread roll'.

Now that you are pregnant, there is probably a host of things you have given up and many lifestyle changes you have made. Don't worry, I am not going to add 'eating out' to the list. Instead, I am going to address some of your most common concerns about eating outside your home, and give you suggestions on how to make it an enjoyable and healthy experience.

'I love going to restaurants. But now that I'm pregnant I have to eat healthy. I constantly worry about what to eat and how it's affecting my baby.'

Most pregnant women find it hard to maintain a balanced diet and eat 'good' healthy food all the time. I know it isn't easy to resist that delicious pasta or baked cannelloni at your favourite restaurant. But this is the time to be mindful of the food you consume. It not only has to be good for your baby but also easy to digest, and should help you to control your weight gain. Occasional indulgences of your favourite meal won't harm your baby. But when these become the rule rather than an exception, take the effort to make better, healthier choices.

Here are some tips to ordering the right meal in restaurants:

*Reading the menu:* A word to the wise: Don't be shy about asking questions or making special requests – 'How do you make this?', 'How much oil do you use?', 'Can I get my fish steamed instead of baked?' Restaurants are used to these. In fact, seeing your condition, most chefs would be eager to please.

*Breaking bread:* Opt for wholegrain or wholewheat bread and pass up on the butter or olive oil. You don't need the extra fat.

*Drink:* Choose fresh fruit juice, coconut water or buttermilk instead of a carbonated drink.

*Salad:* Start with a green or mixed salad with the dressing on the side. Most dressings contain mayonnaise, cream and/or oil – frills you can easily do without. Choose a yoghurt or lemon dressing instead.

*Soup:* Choose a clear vegetable, lentil or bean soup. Avoid creamy soups.

*Main course:*
- ✓ Order protein. If you are non-vegetarian some options are fish or chicken – grilled, broiled, steamed or poached – with the sauce on the side.

✓ Vegetarians could opt for tofu, beans, dal or cottage cheese, or a combination of these.

✓ For a side order, you could opt for vegetables such as sautéed greens, mixed veggies, baked potato or sweet potato.

✓ For your carbs, order fibre-rich options like brown rice, wholewheat pasta, multigrain bread or chapati made from jowar, bajra, wheat, ragi.

*Dessert:* Do you crave something sweet to end your meal? Order a fresh fruit salad instead of rich chocolate mousse or malai kulfi. Bored with fruit? Share the kulfi with your friends. You will be surprised to find that you can eat only a spoon or two after all that food.

## Love to party?

Here are some suggestions to help you continue to be the party animal you were:

✓ Eat a small healthy snack at home before you go to the party. This way you won't gorge on the party snacks.

✓ If you know your host well enough, ask her to make a healthy dish for you.

✓ Take a medium-sized plate. Not only is it easier to hold, it will limit the amount of food you eat.

✓ Eat slowly and enjoy the food. You have a long night ahead.

**Fit tip:** All the meat and fish you order should be thoroughly cooked to avoid parasites and other harmful bacteria. These can cause vomiting, nausea and dehydration, putting you and your baby at risk. Remember, you are more susceptible to food-borne illnesses when you are pregnant.

Eating out is fun, so treat yourself once in a while, without guilt, but choose a restaurant you know and trust. You might crave a particular dish at your favourite restaurant, and I'm not asking you to deny yourself – just be aware of the nutritional value of what you eat. Stick with safe menu choices and indulge yourself, but in moderation. Don't feel like you have to finish everything on your plate. Remember, overeating is worse in your condition. Ask for a doggie bag instead.

## Foods to say 'no' to

Pregnancy is a time for healthy eating. Remember, you are eating for your baby's health too. In this regard you are advised to stay away from certain foods that are potentially hazardous to both you and your unborn child. These are:

**Unpasteurized milk and cheese** made from unpasteurized milk, including some types of mozzarella, blue cheese, feta, Brie or Camembert. Unpasteurized products can cause a bacterial infection called listeriosis, which can cause fever, headache and other serious infections.

Consume pasteurized dairy products that have been refrigerated. Pasteurization is a process that involves heating of milk for a specific duration to destroy bacteria. Unpasteurized juices should also be avoided during pregnancy.

**Street food,** like chaat from roadside stalls, pav bhaji, ragada patties, sandwiches, samosa and kachori, should be avoided. The purity of water and quality of ingredients in these snacks are questionable. Always ensure you consume hygienically prepared food and that the water you drink is clean and pure.

**Unwashed vegetables** can transmit bacterial parasites and cause infections. Wash all vegetables thoroughly; even pre-cut, packaged vegetables should be washed before cooking and eating.

**Raw or undercooked meat** can be detrimental to health as it can cause toxoplasmosis, a parasitic disease, or abdominal pain and diarrhoea due to the presence of E coli bacteria. Toxoplasmosis can result in maternal and foetal infection, leading to premature birth, growth retardation and other complications. While cooking meat, be sure to cook it properly and at a temperature between 70 to 80° C.

**Raw poultry** – chicken and eggs – may contain salmonella, which causes fever, food poisoning, vomiting, diarrhoea and dehydration. All chicken should be cooked to a temperature of 85° C to kill the bacteria. Eggs should be cooked before eating. Avoid products like eggnog and salads that use raw eggs. Pasteurized eggs are best, since the process of pasteurization eliminates the risk of salmonella poisoning. Be sure to maintain proper hygiene; wash utensils thoroughly with hot water and detergent.

**Fish**: Tuna and other large fish contain high levels of mercury. If consumed in large quantities they can cause brain or damage of the nervous system of the foetus. Fish should be well-cooked before consuming.

**Raw sushi, oysters, clams and mussels**: All raw seafood can adversely affect both mother and baby, causing bacterial, parasitic or viral infections. Hence, all raw seafood should be avoided during pregnancy.

# Cravings

*I know it's two in the morning but my wife needs ice-cream please open ...*

'I hear women crave pickle and sour things when they are pregnant. I hate them! Even the smell of pickle makes me nauseous. Is this normal?'

You have been watching too many movies! The fact is, while most pregnant women experience cravings for specific foods – and this may indeed include pickle or sour or spicy foods – they may also have strong aversions to certain foods.

There is a strong belief that food cravings and aversions are your body's way of signalling a need for a particular nutrient or avoiding a potentially harmful food substance. According to this school of thought, women who crave pickles are really craving salt, and may be mineral, specifically sodium, deficient. Though this theory might be true, these signals aren't necessarily reliable and don't seem to follow any particular nutritional pattern. Another popular craving during pregnancy is for ice-cream, mithai, desserts or chocolates, because sugary foods can be associated with comfort. Though you probably won't wake up at 2 a.m. demanding ice-cream, like we see in movies!

**'I'm craving food I never cared for. Everything's going topsy–turvy... food that I've always enjoyed tastes different now. How strange is this?'**

Take heart, this is normal. Most pregnant women say their taste buds undergo a change during pregnancy. Your favourite fruits and vegetables might make you throw up. These sudden and sometimes strange eating habits are most common in your first trimester and can be attributed to your galloping hormones. And anything hormone-related can be extremely confusing.

So which cravings should you ignore and which should you indulge in? The rule of thumb is: if it's a craving for healthy food like fruits and vegetables, indulge to your heart's content. But if it's for something unhealthy like coffee, fried snacks or sweets, read on... you'll find a healthy substitute that will keep your craving and your body happy.

**'How long do cravings last? Is this the cause of my putting on excess weight?'**

You generally start feeling the stirrings of cravings and aversions in the first trimester, but they can start anytime. I don't suggest you stop them, eat whatever you crave – unless it is dangerous to you or your baby – but eat in moderation. Your excess weight gain can be controlled in the second and third trimesters.

In most cases cravings diminish by the fourth month. However, if they do not subside, don't be overly concerned, but do talk to your doctor about them. It might mean that you have some emotional needs that also need to be satisfied. Talk it out it with your husband/partner and bring back that lovin' feeling!

Here are some healthy substitutes to your cravings:

✓ Replace ice-cream with dry fruit, home-made sorbets or flavoured yoghurt.
✓ Instead of mithai, try flavoured yoghurt, sesame laddoo or chikki.
✓ Replace wafers or fried snacks with masala corn cup, corn on the cob, baked chips or popcorn.
✓ Limit chocolate and mithai intake to a small piece at a time.
✓ Instead of cola, drink fresh coconut water or plain water.

## Bizarre cravings

'I think I'm losing my mind... I crave pickles, ice-cream and even chalk! What is wrong with me?'

No, you aren't going crazy! I've interacted with enough pregnant women to say this with the utmost confidence. Pregnancy can be a challenging time for a mommy-to-be. Often sugar and fat metabolism are affected during pregnancy, so the most common cravings are for foods containing fat and sugar. But pregnant women experience bizarre food cravings too.

| Common cravings | Unusual cravings* |
|---|---|
| Pickles | Clay |
| Ice-cream | Mud |
| Salted snacks | Ash |
| Aerated drinks | Chalk |
| Sweets | Soap |

* This craving for unusual substances like chalk, clay and ash is called pica. It could be due to hormonal disturbances. Consult your doctor if the condition persists.

## Smell

'I used to love my husband's perfume; it made me go weak in the knees. Now it makes me sick to the stomach. Is this related to my pregnancy?'

Alas, yes, along with an unusual sense of taste you may also experience an altered sense of smell. The aromas and fragrances you loved in the past can be distasteful during pregnancy. Some pregnant women find that strong odours can trigger morning sickness as well. Assure your husband that the romance isn't dead, just asleep! Your senses should go back to normal after the baby is born.

How to deal with strong odours:

✓  Pack away any offending perfume, soap or shampoo.
✓  Avoid cooking food with strong aromas like garlic, onions and fish.
✓  While cooking, turn on the exhaust fan and open a window.
✓  Cooking strong smelling foods in the oven may help minimize the odour.

## Food FAQs

In this section I have addressed some of your concerns and answered some of the most frequently asked questions about food in pregnancy. These answers have been compiled after extensive research to give you the best information available.

*Q: I'm a vegetarian. Do I have to eat animal products to have a healthy baby?*

Don't believe everything you hear. Vegetarians can certainly have healthy babies, otherwise more than half the women out there would suffer! You just have to take extra care in planning your diet and consult your doctor about taking supplements in case you need them.

Tips for choosing your menu:

✓ *Protein:* For ovo-lacto-vegetarians, protein could be obtained from eggs and milk products. For vegans, dried beans, peas, lentils, tofu and other soya products could help satisfy your protein requirement.

✓ *Calcium:* For ovo-lacto-vegetarians, this could be obtained from dairy products. For vegans, calcium-fortified juices, dark green leafy vegetables, sesame seeds, almonds and soya products such as soya milk, soya cheese and tofu are good for the diet.

✓ *Vitamin B12:* Although B12 deficiencies are rare, vegetarians and vegans in particular may not get enough of this vitamin in their daily diet. They can supplement their requirement with B12 fortified soya milk and cereals.

### Q: Is it dangerous to drink unpasteurized milk?

Pasteurization destroys harmful bacteria. To ensure that you and your baby are protected from harmful bacterial infections such as listeria, consume pasteurized milk. In fact, you should make sure all the dairy products you consume are made from pasteurized milk. Today even eggs are available in pasteurized form, so opt for these whenever possible.

### Q: What are the sources of protein for a vegetarian?

Vegetarians can get their supply of protein from pulses and grains, milk and milk products and soya products. But animal sources, such as milk and milk products, are complete sources of protein while vegetable sources are incomplete. Hence, vegetable protein needs to be consumed in combination with other foods to be complete. For example, combine grains and lentils (dal and chapati/rice) or grains and nuts or beans.

Here are some excellent sources of vegetarian protein which provide approximately the same amount of protein as an ounce of meat:

> ¼ cup cottage cheese or paneer
> 1 egg – limit egg yolk consumption to three per
>    week as it is high in cholesterol
> ½ cup cooked legumes/lentils
> 1 cup soya milk
> 2 tbsp mixed nuts
> 2 tbsp peanut butter
> 1 cup yoghurt/milk
> 2 inch piece of hard cheese
> ½ cup cooked beans (rajma, channa)

### Q: I hear tofu is very good for vegetarians. What exactly is tofu?

Tofu is produced by grinding cooked soya beans to make a milky substance that can be solidified. It is also known as soya bean curd. Its naturally bland properties render it easy to use in sweet or savoury dishes.

Tofu is excellent for you as it is high in protein and low in saturated fats. A 100 gram serving of tofu contains 73 calories. Firm tofu is low in fat while softer tofu tends to have a higher fat content. It is also cholesterol free.

It can be found in most supermarkets and food stores.

**Fit fact:** Soya is the only plant food that contains all nine essential amino acids in sufficient proportions to be considered a complete protein.

*Q: Can I continue my low-carb and high-protein diet during my pregnancy?*

Pregnancy is not a time for dieting! Carbohydrates are your body's main source of energy. Your red blood cells and brain cells depend on them for their energy requirements. If you give up or restrict carbs, your body has to derive its energy needs from the breakdown of muscle protein or muscle tissue, causing you to lose healthy muscle tissue. You also need complex carbohydrates to give you vital fibre and vitamin B, which help ward off constipation and morning sickness.

Trying to restrict any of the essential nutrients is not the right way to go, especially when you are pregnant. Refer to my chapter on 'A Square Meal' to learn how to eat right and get all the nutrition you need during pregnancy.

*Q: What are good fats?*

Examples of good fats are monounsaturated fats found in oils such as sesame, olive, groundnut and canola oil. Polyunsaturated fats from plant sources such as corn and sunflower are also beneficial. When consumed in small quantities, they work to reduce blood cholesterol levels and protect you against heart disease.

> **Lipids** are fats that are found throughout the body. Cholesterol, a type of lipid, is found in animal sources of food. Eggs, meat and whole-fat dairy products (including milk, cheese and ice-cream) are loaded with cholesterol; vegetables, fruits and grains contain none. Cholesterol is necessary for foetal development. The pregnant woman's body automatically increases the production of cholestrol, raising blood cholesterol levels anywhere from 25 to 40 per cent.

*Q: My mother-in-law is constantly feeding me food and sweets cooked in ghee. She insists it is good for me and my baby. Is this true?*

This is a constant lament among many of my clients, especially those who live in joint families. In India, traditional cooking methods rely heavily on ghee and home-made butter. In fact, there is a school of thought that believes food cooked in ghee is healthy and tastes better. However, everything must be enjoyed in moderation. Limit the ghee and sugar consumption to avoid piling on excess calories, and keep enjoying your mother-in-law's attention.

*Q: I am losing a lot of hair; is this because of a poor diet?*

The major causes of hair fall are pollution and chemicals but you could blame a poor diet too. Losing hair in excess could be the result of iron, zinc or protein deficiency. In women, in particular, the most common reason for hair fall is anaemia or lack of iron.

But take heart, hair fall due to nutritional deficiencies can be corrected; so the sooner you get back to a balanced diet the better! Make sure your diet is enriched with the following foods to give your scalp the nutrition it needs:

✓ For iron, consume iron-rich food like dates, figs, prunes, raisins and beetroot.
✓ For zinc, eat peanuts, pulses, eggs and wholegrain cereals.
✓ For protein, include dairy products, pulses, sprouts, nuts, seeds, soya and fish in your diet.

*Q: Milk makes me uncomfortable; I feel queasy every time I drink it. How important is it for my baby? Are there any alternatives?*

The reason doctors recommend milk during pregnancy is because it is considered the finest and most convenient source of protein and calcium in the diet. You can consume up to three glasses of milk every day during pregnancy for your increased calcium and protein needs. But, more than milk, your baby needs the calcium derived from milk to fulfil its nutritional needs. If you are lactose intolerant, try these substitutes:

✓ If you can stomach some kinds of dairy products, try paneer or yoghurt (the active cultures aid in digestion) or lactose-free milk.

✓ If you are allergic to these, try consuming calcium-fortified juices, non-dairy calcium and protein-rich foods. Or consult your doctor about taking a calcium supplement.

✓ If you simply don't like the taste of milk, cleverly mask it in cereals, soups and smoothies.

**Q: I love sushi and eat it all the time; can I continue to eat it during pregnancy?**

Sorry, you will have to do without your favourite food while you are pregnant. Seafood contains mercury, and when it isn't cooked it can make you sick – not worth the risk when you're pregnant. So avoid all raw fish or shellfish like sushi, sashimi, raw oysters, clams, fish tartars. But don't despair! You can safely enjoy other healthy Japanese offerings with cooked fish or seafood and vegetables.

**Q: I like my food spicy. Is this safe during pregnancy?**

Indian food tends to be spicy. Eating spicy food during pregnancy is not harmful to you or your baby. Just make sure you can stomach any indigestion or heartburn that can result from eating all that hot food. In fact, all chillies and peppers are considered extremely nutritious, since they contain vitamin C. So as long as these foods agree with your digestive system, eat without risk.

*Q: I ate out last night and then threw up a lot. Will this harm my baby?*

You may have suffered from food poisoning. This affects you more than your baby. After all, you're the one who vomited. The main concern is dehydration. Your body loses fluids so make sure you consume adequate liquids such as water, coconut water or fresh lime water to stay well hydrated through the day. Contact your doctor for further recommendations.

*Q: I love sweets and can't seem to get enough. Are sweeteners harmful during pregnancy?*

The verdict is still awaited on whether sugar substitutes are completely safe to use during pregnancy. Always consult your doctor before use, and use in moderation.

*Q: Is it safe to drink herbal tea during pregnancy?*

Sure, the world is switching to herbal tea. But what effect herbs have on pregnant women is still a grey area. Chamomile tea is known to be safe and helps soothe an upset stomach. Seek your doctor's advice on what suits you.

## To believe or not to believe: pregnancy myths debunked

This is a time in your life when everyone you meet, even total strangers on the internet, will give you advice. 'Do this, don't do this,' or 'eat that, don't eat that'. You will hear these words more often when you are pregnant than at any other time in your life.

Everyone from your friends and relatives to your colleagues and neighbours has an opinion. When the advice contains facts you can use, that's good; but when it's just myths and urban legends, that is the last thing you need at this time.

Don't believe everything you are told. Take everything with the proverbial 'pinch of salt'. In most cases you will need a whole bagful!

To help clear the confusion, I am going to address the most common pregnancy beliefs and misconceptions, some of the worst fears and concerns that have been around for generations. Your mother and grandmother were plagued by them and, doubtless, your children will be too. That's just the world we live in. I am going to help you differentiate fact from fiction, between age-old myths in the guise of 'wisdom' and modern scientific facts and breakthroughs.

*Myth. When you're pregnant, you're eating for two, so have double portions of everything.*
Definitely not! Your appetite may increase substantially, but your actual caloric requirements are only marginally increased. Your baby doesn't need many calories to develop. You need just 300 extra calories a day to meet your pregnancy needs. As long as you eat three square meals a day and 3 to 5 mini meals, as per the guidelines I've suggested, and your doctor is happy with your progress, you and your baby will be fine.

*Myth. Consume ample ghee to ease the delivery process.*
Ghee, butter and oil are fattening, and their consumption should be restricted. Excess consumption can create unnecessary health problems and can make you gain extra weight. Overweight pregnancies have higher complications and difficult labours. Your mother or mother-in-law may want to fatten you up to ensure a 'healthier' baby. But this is an old wives' tale and should

be ignored. Appreciate the concern but say 'no thanks!' Instead, continue your regular physical activities and exercise to tone your body as this will prove to be helpful during labour and delivery.

**Myth.** *Eating sweets such as laddoos and barfis provides the baby with much needed energy.*
You shouldn't be consuming too many sweets as they are high in calories. Too much sugar will make you obese and could also lead to gestational diabetes, which is harmful.

**Myth.** *Spicy foods induce labour.*
Remember Rachel in *Friends* gorging on jalapeño peppers to induce labour? Just as it didn't work for her, it's not going to work for you. Pregnant women can eat most spices, but there are certain foods that you are advised to avoid, such as ajinomoto (MSG), unpasteurized dairy and raw fish.

**Myth.** *Eating papaya leads to abortion.*
This is a universal myth; perhaps the papaya's capacity to aid bowel movement gives the impression that it will carry the foetus down somehow. However, there is no scientific evidence to support this. Taken in moderation, papaya causes no harm; in fact, it helps in countering constipation, if you suffer from it.

**Myth.** *Citrus foods aggravate acidity.*
Citrus fruits are known to cause acidity in some women, so if you face this problem, do avoid them. However, if you do not suffer from acidity, continue to eat these fruits as they are good sources of vitamin C and fibre, and are highly recommended during pregnancy.

**Myth.** *'Heating food in the microwave is harmful to the baby.*
No good science shows that microwaves harm the foetus. You are safe.

## Taboos

Certain substances like alcohol and certain habits like smoking and taking recreational drugs are considered taboo, especially during pregnancy. In fact, we are still learning about the harmful effects these substances can have on you and your baby.

It's better to be safe than sorry. There is a precious life growing inside you that is dependent on you for its existence. Your number one priority over the next nine months should be taking care of yourself, so you can take care of your baby.

### Alcohol

Maternal alcohol consumption can be associated with a condition known as foetal alcohol syndrome. The main features of these conditions range from poor growth, trouble with learning and attention, to more severe mental retardation. According to the statistics, this syndrome occurs in 30 to 40 per cent women who consume alcohol during pregnancy. That's why doctors and gynaecologists the world over maintain a strict 'no alcohol' policy during pregnancy.

**'I've heard it's okay to have an occasional glass of wine during pregnancy.'**

At one time it was believed that an occasional glass of wine was okay. But since then, it has been thought that alcohol is probably the greatest single cause of birth defects. Even one can of beer or a glass of wine could have an impact on the development of your unborn child. So until more is known, complete abstinence is the safest way to go. If you drink regularly, or have trouble quitting on your own, get help before becoming pregnant or as soon as you know you're pregnant.

**'I drank regularly before I found out I was pregnant. Could this harm my baby?'**

This is a common concern, but rest assured there is no evidence that a few drinks consumed early in pregnancy will harm a developing embryo. Continuing to drink throughout your pregnancy, however, could result in the wide range of problems explained above.

Every drink a pregnant woman takes is consumed by her baby as well. Since it takes the baby more time to eliminate the alcohol from its system, the baby can be highly intoxicated when the mother is just about starting to enjoy her drink.

If you were indulging before you discovered you were expecting, I would advise you not to obsess over it now. Letting it consume you with guilt or allowing it to become a source of undue stress is bad for you and your baby. Instead, focus your energy on living a healthy lifestyle now for the remainder of your term, and into your breastfeeding period.

## Smoking

*Smoking kills! Tobacco causes cancer.*

Every cigarette packet carries these statutory warnings. Smoking has become a universal taboo, whether you are pregnant or not. Smoking in public places – offices, restaurants, even bars and pubs – is banned by law in most countries. How much more warning do you need?

It is an established fact that, apart from exposing you to cardiovascular disease, lung cancer and high blood pressure, smoking can also have dire consequences for your baby. Therefore, women who smoke place their child at great risk. Among the more serious of these are premature placental detachment, rupture of the membranes and premature delivery.

**'Will the many cigarettes I have smoked in the past adversely affect my baby?'**

The good news is that any smoking you've done in the past will not harm your baby. But smoking during pregnancy is harmful to both you and the baby. So if you're a smoker, quitting now can make a big difference to your baby's health. You now have greater motivation to kick that butt!

Studies have shown that babies born to women who quit smoking early in their pregnancy had birth weights that were almost 300 grams higher than those who did not. Also, the baby feels suffocated because of insufficient oxygen, and this can increase the baby's heart rate and adversely affect its growth.

If you continue to smoke despite all the warnings, you may have to live with the guilt in case complications arise. Further, statistics suggest that if a parent smokes, a child is more likely to become a smoker too – not the kind of legacy you want to leave to your child.

Bottom line: Smoking, actively or passively, is not only bad for your health, it is bad for your baby as well.

## Recreational drugs: cocaine, heroin, marijuana

Drug use can result in premature labour, low birth weight and dangerous birth complications in which the placenta separates from the uterus prematurely.

Research suggests that children exposed to drug use in the

womb have lower IQ scores as well as learning, emotional and behavioural problems.

So you've had a wild past, Concentrate on your present and future now. Find healthier ways to relax and unwind. Start setting a good example right away.

# FITNESS

Better to hunt in fields, for health unbought,
Than fee the doctor for a nauseous draught,
The wise, for cure, on exercise depend;
God never made his work for man to mend.
                                    – John Dryden

# Exercise
## Boon or Bane?

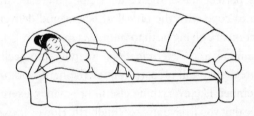

Anybody who knows me knows I am a great proponent of exercise. I think exercise is a great way to stay in shape and feel good about yourself at any time, and even more so when you are having a baby. Right about now you're probably thinking, 'What is she talking about?'

Let me tell you some of the common concerns that my clients have. I am certain similar queries are on your mind too.

**'I'm aching all over, I can't sleep and my back is killing me. My ankles are swollen and I feel bloated. Some days it's extremely hard to get up and get dressed for work. What can I do to feel better?'**

If you, like many other pregnant women, are suffering from the side effects of pregnancy and are willing to try anything for some relief, here's the answer – EXERCISE!

Don't just take my word for it, ask your doctor. She will tell you that women with normal pregnancies should get 30 minutes or more moderate exercise per day. More and more women are taking this advice and making fitness a part of their daily routine. It doesn't matter if you haven't exercised since high school, there's plenty to be gained from exercising.

**'I had heard horror stories about labour and delivery and was terrified about giving birth. I started exercising to prepare myself both physically and mentally for D-Day. And it worked. I hardly felt a thing!'**

It makes perfect sense: the better shape you're in, the better you'll be to cope with the ordeal of labour and delivery. Some women compare giving birth to running a marathon – it requires focus, stamina and determination. Keeping physically active during pregnancy will prepare you for the hard work of labour. But remember, like everything else in pregnancy, exercise can't guarantee that you'll have an easy childbirth. However, experience tells us that mothers who exercise tend to have shorter labour and are less likely to need labour and delivery interventions including C-section. In addition, research shows us that women who exercise may tolerate labour better than those who don't.

## Benefits of exercise

### For you

Regular exercise improves:

### Stamina

**'Too much rest can make you feel more tired.'**

Paradox? But it's true! Try lying around the whole day and you will find it even harder to get up. Pregnancy can rob you of energy, but a little exercise – even a 10 minute stroll – can go a long way in giving your energy level the boost it needs. Regular exercise strengthens your cardiovascular system, making it easier to tackle your daily chores and feel less tired doing it.

## Sleep

**'I have a hard time falling asleep... and when I do it's never for more than 4 to 5 hours.'**

This is a common grouse with many pregnant women. When you're carrying all that extra weight, finding a comfortable position to sleep in can be a real challenge. Again, the answer is exercise. Regular exercise will help you work off any excess energy and will tire you enough to fall into a deeper sleep, and you will wake up feeling more rested and refreshed.

## Health

Exercise may prevent gestational diabetes, a growing problem among pregnant women.

## Mood

At the best of times, these nine months can feel like an ordeal. After the initial excitement of discovering you're having a baby dies down, it is one discomfort after another all the way. By the time you roll into your third trimester, you are either bored out of your mind because it is cramping your social life, or tearing your hair out waiting for it to be over. What you need is exercise. Remember, exercise causes your brain to release endorphins, the 'feel-good' chemicals that give you a natural high, improving your mood and diminishing stress and anxiety.

## Self-image

**'My figure's gone; I look as big as a house, people give me a wide berth when I walk by.'**

Alas, your body is not the svelte sexy thing it used to be. But don't be disheartened; despite what the weighing scale says, it is only temporary and the outcome is definitely worth it. Find an activity that's fun and appropriate for you. Staying active can improve your self-image and make you feel less ungainly.

## Back

Exercise will help you develop a strong set of abs, which can relieve back pain and pressure.

## Stiffness

Exercise stretches and strengthens your muscles, helping your body cope better with the aches and pains of pregnancy. Stretching is particularly good for your body. It can help ward off sore muscles, and the best part – you can do it anytime, anywhere!

## Bowels

An active body encourages active bowels. Even a 10 minute walk can help get things moving in the right direction.

## Postpartum recovery

The fitter you stay during pregnancy, the faster you will recover physically after childbirth, and the faster you will get into your pre-pregnancy jeans. For most women, this is reason enough to climb on the exercise train. Remember, if you maintain your strength and muscle tone throughout your pregnancy, you will find it easier to bounce back to your pre-pregnancy weight and figure after delivery.

## For your baby

Research suggests that changes in heart rate and oxygen levels in exercising mothers-to-be stimulate their babies. Your unborn child can also be influenced by the sounds and vibrations she experiences in the womb during your workout. Thus, if you exercise regularly during pregnancy, your baby might end up being:

*More fit.* Babies of mothers who exercise during pregnancy are born at healthier weights, are less traumatized by labour and delivery, and recover from the stresses of birth more quickly.

*More relaxed.* Babies of exercising mothers tend to sleep through the night, are less prone to colic and are better able to soothe themselves.

## Exercise safety: dos and don'ts

Pregnant women and women planning a baby inundate me with questions about fitness during pregnancy. Is exercising safe? How much exercise is good? How much is too much? What are the signs that I'm overdoing it? What should I avoid?

While exercise can be a boon to you and your baby, here are some basic dos and don'ts that you should follow to ensure that you stay healthy and safe.

### Do...

### Consult your doctor

The MOST important thing to remember: once you decide on an exercise programme, discuss it with your doctor and get her approval. Even if you are feeling healthy and are anxious to get started you must be declared medically fit before embarking on any exercise regimen. If you followed an exercise programme before pregnancy, discuss it with your doctor. Chances are, you can continue it in modified form, through your pregnancy.

## Start slow

Like everything else in pregnancy, easy does it! Resist the urge to start off with a bang, like working out for an hour, twice a day. This enthusiasm can not only be dangerous but can lead to a host of exercise blues like sore muscles, stiffness and a reluctance to continue exercising.

> If you are a beginner, this is the ideal workout plan:
> - Start with 5 minutes warm up
> - Continue with 10 minutes moderate workout
> - End with 5 minutes cool down

Once your body starts adjusting to the workout, increase the duration of the exercises gradually.

## Finish slow

Your body must be allowed to cool down after any form of exercise. For example, walk after you run, paddle after a vigorous swim, and do some light stretching after any activity. Finish off your cool down with a few minutes of relaxation. Stopping exercise abruptly traps blood in the muscles, reducing blood supply to other parts of your body, including your baby. This could lead to dizziness, faintness, elevated heartbeat and/ or even nausea.

## Time watch

Exercising too little is not effective; exercising too much can be debilitating. A complete workout from warm up to cool down can average 30 minutes to an hour. Ensure that the period of strenuous exercise does not exceed 15 minutes.

## Be consistent

Exercise regularly – 5 to 7 days a week – for best results and optimum health. Remember, irregular exercise is not effective and won't keep you in shape.

Most of my clients agree that once you start your exercise routine, you feel better if you do some exercise every day.

## Make time for it

The best way to ensure that you exercise regularly is to allot a specific time for it: first thing in the morning, afternoon, or before dinner. Working women should build it into their schedule: walk to work, exercise at lunch time or go for a walk after dinner.

## Consume adequate calories

You will need an additional 100 to 200 calories to compensate for the calories you burn during exercise. If you are consuming the extra calories and still not gaining the required amount of weight, you could be overdoing the exercise.

## Eat a healthy snack

Consume a cereal and protein snack at least one hour before you exercise.

Good examples of energy foods are sprouts or cottage cheese in wholegrain bread, nuts and fruits with low-fat milk.

## Stay hydrated

Be sure to drink plenty of fluids before, during and after exercise to prevent dehydration. For every 30 minutes of strenuous activity you need at least one glass of extra liquid to compensate for fluids lost due to perspiration.

## Dress right

Wear loose clothes that allow for unrestricted movement and stretching. Opt for light cotton fabrics that let your body breathe during exercise. Invest in a pair of well-fitting athletic shoes to protect your feet.

## Find the right surface

Indoors: Opt for wood floors or a tightly carpeted surface rather than bare tiles or concrete.

Outdoors: Soft or grassy running tracks are better than hard surfaced roads and pavements. Avoid uneven surfaces.

## Know your limit

Exercise should make you feel exhilarated, not exhausted. Check for signs of pain or strain on any part of your body, profuse sweating, or breathlessness – these mean that you are overdoing it and need to slow down.

## Listen to your body

If it doesn't feel right, it probably isn't. Your body will signal when it is time to modify or stop any exercise or movement that causes extreme discomfort. Signals to watch out for are: pain anywhere, a cramp or stitch, lightheadedness or dizziness, palpitations, severe breathlessness, difficulty walking or loss of muscle control, a headache, increased swelling of your hands, feet, ankles or face.

If any of these symptoms aren't relieved by a short rest, call your doctor.

## Stay cool

Minimise exercise in very hot and humid weather. Research has shown that exercises or environments that raise your temperature by more than 1.5 to 2°F are dangerous, since the blood gets shunted away from the uterus to the skin in an attempt to cool the body. Exercise in cool, airy rooms at cooler times of the day.

## Be safe

During pregnancy, your centre of gravity shifts forward with the uterus, affecting your sense of balance, hence you should take care to avoid back strain.

Be aware of the added risk of injury due to lax joints caused by hormonal changes. Drop exercises that could compromise your safety – like walking, jogging or cycling on wet surfaces, or any activity that requires sudden movement.

## Slow down in the third trimester

In the last three months of pregnancy, you should consider winding down all other activities including exercising. Stay with low-impact exercises such as walking, cycling, swimming and light yoga as you prepare for the big event – childbirth.

## Don't…

## Work out on an empty stomach

While the old rule of not swimming after a meal is true, it is equally hazardous to exercise on an empty stomach. Make it a practice to have a snack and drink an hour or two before exercising.

## Hold your breath

You must breathe freely and deeply during exercise.

## Make jerky or jarring movements

Any jerky, jarring or twisting movement puts additional stress on your joints and parts of your body that are already overloaded by the increased weight of your pregnancy.

## Lie on your back

It is not advisable to lie on your back after the third month of pregnancy as the weight of your enlarging uterus could constrict major blood vessels, restricting circulation. If you are lying on your back and experience symptoms such as dizziness, nausea or shortness of breath, roll onto your left side to re-establish blood flow.

## Cause trauma to the abdominal area

Avoid any exercise or activity that could cause trauma to your abdominal area; for instance, stay away from contact sports such as cricket, football and basketball and recreational activities like skiing, horseback riding, gymnastics and scuba diving.

## Exercise for weight loss

Exercise during pregnancy is to promote the health and well-being of both you and your baby. In fact, you are encouraged to put on the right amount of weight at the right time. Staying fit during pregnancy will improve your chances of losing the excess weight after delivery.

## Contraindications

Doctors may advise women with certain conditions to do very little or no exercise. If you suffer from or have suffered from any of these conditions, you should always check with your doctor before starting any exercise programme.

The following conditions require medical guidance and supervision:

✓ Spotting or bleeding
✓ Diabetes
✓ Thyroid disease
✓ Anaemia or other blood disorders
✓ A foetus that is seriously over- or underweight.
✓ If you lead an extremely sedentary lifestyle

Exercise is NOT advised in these conditions:

✓ A history of spontaneous miscarriages
✓ Premature labour
✓ Multiple pregnancy
✓ An incompetent cervix
✓ A diagnosis of placenta praevia
✓ Heart disease
✓ High blood pressure
✓ Ruptured membranes

## Know your exercise personality

As someone once said, to really motivate people, you need to engage their minds and their hearts. So before you start any exercise routine, ask yourself: what is your exercise personality? What do you enjoy doing? If you start an exercise programme half-heartedly, you're not going to continue with it for long. So find out what makes you tick.

Take for instance my client Poonam – when she discovered she was pregnant, she started going for a walk in the park with her two best friends. They would catch up on the day's events and the latest gossip. After one month she found it so monotonous that she stopped. But Poonam knew she needed some form of exercise to avoid feeling hot and bothered and lethargic all the time. She decided to accompany her husband to his club – he played tennis and she enrolled in swimming lessons. It was exhilarating to be in the water. Soon she was hooked. The added bonus – she and her husband would have a hearty breakfast at the club after their exercise.

Here's what some of my other clients had to say about their preferences. If any of these resonate with you, it's great! If not, find your exercise personality. You must enjoy your exercise plan if you want to turn your motivation into a lifelong habit.

Meenal gets her fix by attending group pregnancy classes. Being with and talking to other pregnant women is her 'constructive timeout'. 'I love participating in group exercise classes. The enthusiasm of the group keeps my energy levels high.'

Sonia, on the other hand, prefers to work out alone. 'I am surrounded by people all day at work so I long for some alone time. Give me a good pair of sneakers and my iPod and I'm out of the house! I love being on my own and nothing beats the freedom of a brisk walk...'

Pooja prefers the calmness of yoga. 'The peace and quiet, the balance between my mind and my body is what I want... yoga and pranayama relax and rejuvenate me.'

There are a lot of safe activities that could be taken up during pregnancy:

- ✓ Walking
- ✓ Swimming
- ✓ Cycling – on a stationary bicycle
- ✓ Aqua aerobics
- ✓ Stretching
- ✓ Strength training
- ✓ Yoga
- ✓ Pre-natal exercise classes

## Getting started

**'I have never exercised before. I'm extremely nervous, where do I start? What exercises should I do now that I am pregnant?'**

Don't be unduly stressed. As I tell all my pregnant clients, this can be a great time to get active, even if you haven't exercised before. Rest assured there are many good reasons to make exercise a part of your daily routine.

However, the most important thing to remember is to exercise with caution. The extra weight you are carrying will make your body work harder than before. It is not an exaggeration to say that a pregnant woman's body is in a constant state of work, so stop exercising when you are tired and do not exercise to the point of exhaustion.

Many start an exercise programme with a great deal of enthusiasm, but fail to sustain the momentum. This is often due to mental and physical burn-out.

Take the case of Maya – when she became pregnant at 22, she was extremely overweight. Her gynaecologist recommended exercise for a healthier pregnancy. Maya dove headlong into her exercise routine. She would walk briskly for 45 minutes every morning at a nearby park, and walk on the treadmill for an hour every evening. Soon she found it very hard to continue pushing her tired body to this level of exertion and could not sustain her motivation. The result: she stopped exercising altogether.

Always begin at a level that is right for you and then progress sensibly. Listen to your body and exercise with caution. For most pregnant women, 30 minutes of moderate exercise is recommended on most, if not all, days of the week. But even shorter and less frequent workouts can help you stay in shape and prepare for labour.

Walking is a great exercise for beginners. It provides moderate aerobic conditioning with minimal stress on your joints. Other good choices include swimming and cycling on a stationary bike. Strength training is good too, as long as you avoid lifting heavy weights.

If you have not exercised for a while, you can begin with as little as 20 minutes of walking, increasing it to 25 minutes until you can manage 30 minutes a day. Remember to drink plenty of fluids to stay hydrated and be careful to avoid excessive heat.

## Motivation

'When I read about the benefits of exercising, I got really excited and decided to do it the very next day. But when the time came to follow through, my motivation suddenly disappeared. I sat back, feeling too lethargic to move.'

I work out for one and a half hours! Fifteen minutes of cardio, 15 minutes of stretching and one hour of motivating myself.

If this sounds like you, it's time to focus your attention on what's important. Deciding to exercise is important, but it's what you do to follow through that really matters.

Motivation is a crucial factor in any exercise regimen. Without motivation, giving up is easy. Slacking off for a day can turn into slacking off for a week, a month and eventually quitting the programme altogether. The key is to find the right exercise for you. If it is fun, you are more likely to stay motivated.

Try the following pop quiz I give all my clients when they join my exercise class.

## Are you motivated to exercise?

Answer YES or NO

1. Do you consider exercise an integral part of your life?
2. Are you able to stick to your exercise programme?
3. Do you enjoy working out?
4. Do you feel an exercise programme would make you more confident?
5. Do you pay attention to correct exercise techniques when you work out?
6. Does exercise improve your mood and help you cope better with stress?
7. Does exercise increase your energy levels?

If you have answered 'Yes' to at least five of these questions, you are on track. If not, you have some work to do. But there is no need to despair, just read on.

It is important to remember that motivation does not just happen. It is something you make happen, each and every day. If you have multiple reasons to exercise, you will always have something to get you moving. The hardest part of exercise is getting started; if you can get that far, you've won half the battle.

Tips for staying motivated:

✓ *Start small.* You do not need to join a gym or buy expensive workout clothes to get in shape. Just get moving. Take a daily walk through your neighbourhood. Vary your route to keep it interesting.

✓ *Buddy up.* Don't like walking alone? Ask a friend to join you. Exercise can be more interesting if you use the time to chat. Better yet, involve your husband/partner and catch up on the day's events.

✓ *Got music? Get ready to rumble!* Make exercise fun. Listen to music or watch TV while you exercise. Soon you'll be walking to your own beat.

✓ *Take a prenatal class.* Many fitness centres offer classes designed for pregnant women. Choose one that fits your interests and schedule.

✓ *Get creative.* Vary your routine. You are less likely to get bored if you change your exercise routine. Walk one day, bicycle the next, swim on the third and so on.

✓ *Rest when you need to.* Be aware of your body at all times. Alter your workout intensity as your pregnancy progresses. Your tolerance for strenuous exercise will probably decrease as your pregnancy progresses.

## Exercise planning

An ideal exercise plan ensures that your entire body and mind get the workout they need. While conducting prenatal exercise classes, I vary the different forms of exercise for each day of the week. It includes exercises that build stamina, strength and suppleness and also encourages the practice of deep breathing and relaxation.

For an effective exercise plan, I recommend:

✓ Walking/swimming/aqua aerobics/cycling: 3 to 5 days a week
✓ Yoga/stretching/strength training: 2 to 3 days a week
✓ Deep breathing and relaxation: 7 days a week

Decide on an exercise routine you enjoy and one that suits you best.

You could use the following tips on scheduling your exercise for optimum benefits.

## Time watch

Exercising too little is not effective; exercising too much can be debilitating. A complete workout from warm up to cool down can average 20 minutes to an hour.

If you are accustomed to intense exercise, ensure that, during pregnancy, the period of strenuous exercise does not exceed 15 minutes at a time. Also, always check with your gynaecologist for any specific exercise recommendations.

## Divide and conquer

'I can't cope with exercising for one hour at a stretch. I get too tired. What can I do to ensure I'm getting the exercise I need?'

Firstly, you are exercising during pregnancy to stay fit and active during pregnancy; not training for a marathon (though it often feels like it!). Normal rules of exercise don't apply to you now.

A 60 minute workout session can easily be split into three sessions of 20 minutes each, spread over the morning, afternoon and evening. Short spurts of exercise also count during pregnancy. They have been shown to provide similar benefits to longer workouts. You can spot-march in place or cycle on an exercise cycle while watching your favourite movie or TV show.

## Make time

Work exercise into your schedule. The best way to ensure that you exercise regularly is to allot a specific time for it.

## How often?

Exercise needs to be regular for it to be effective. I recommend 3 to 7 days a week. Vary your routine, like I have suggested earlier; give your muscles time to recover. Once you get started, you will find that you feel better if you exercise for some time every day.

## How hard?

If you can't hold a conversation while exercising, slow down. Try the 'talk test' – a method used for measuring exercise intensity. In general, if you are able to carry on a light conversation while exercising, you are working out at a low-to-moderate pace. If you are breathless or if your speech starts to break or causes discomfort, you are working out at a harder, more intense pace, which is generally not recommended during pregnancy.

## How much rest?

Adequate rest is absolutely vital for growth and development. It helps the muscles to recuperate from the stresses of exercise and helps the body get rid of fatigue and muscular exhaustion. Especially during weight training, the muscles need at least 48 hours of rest between workout sessions to recover and rejuvenate.

## When to stop?

I can't stress this enough – trust your body's signals. Your body will tell you when it's time to stop. Listen to it. Call you doctor if there is the slightest doubt.

## Move out of positions slowly

If you get out of exercise positions too fast you will feel dizzy and might hurt yourself. Support yourself, especially when moving from a lying down position to a standing position.

The proper technique for getting up from a lying position:

A:  Roll onto your left side

B:  With the help of your hands, slowly push yourself to a sitting position.

## Exercise basics

No exercise plan is complete without what I call the 'exercise basics' – walking, swimming or cycling.

'Sometimes when I'm in a real hurry and running late for work, I jump on my stationary bicycle and cycle for 20 minutes. Then I shower and run out of the door.'

If you have 20 minutes, the correct practice would be: warm up for 5 minutes by bicycling at an easy pace; increase intensity for 10 minutes; and cool down by tapering off intensity for the last 5 minutes.

If you find yourself in a time crunch, my advice is to exercise correctly within the time you have allocated for your workout. Without a proper warm up and cool down, not only is your exercise routine incomplete, but you could also cause injury to your body.

Here is why.

## Warm up

Just as a cold car engine has to warm up before it can perform, your body too has to warm up before it can start working to full capability. Remember, especially when pregnant, you need to start slowly and gradually build up the workout intensity.

What exactly does a warm up do? A warm up prepares the body physically and mentally for the exercises to follow and also improves the effectiveness of the exercise. It gradually elevates your heart rate, enabling the oxygen in your blood to travel at greater speed, and boosts circulation. It increases the temperature in the muscles, improving muscle elasticity and reducing the risk of strains and pulls. A warm up should include about 5 to 10 minutes of light activity, such as walking, spot-marching or knee lifts.

## Cool down

Equally important is the cool down process. The main aim of the cool down is to promote recovery and return the body gradually to a pre-exercise level. During a strenuous workout, your body goes through a number of stressful processes. The cool down, when performed properly, assists your body in its recovery, repair and regeneration. If you cut off exercise abruptly, without a cool down period, it can result in a rapid drop in blood pressure. You may also suffer from cramps, muscle soreness and lightheadedness.

'When I first started exercising I would feel so stiff the next day. It was extremely painful to walk down the stairs because my legs felt so sore.'

Too much, too fast or too soon causes pain and severe muscle soreness. Your objective should be to gradually prepare your body for exercise without over-training or over-straining. Make sure your exercise programme is structured, systematic and progressive.

## The 3 S's of fitness: a guide to the three basic forms of exercise

Stamina, suppleness and strength or, as I like to call them, the '3 S's of fitness' are the basic forms of exercise. An ideal exercise regimen should incorporate all of these. Say, for example, you are a walking enthusiast – you can walk to build your stamina; you can improve your suppleness by stretching or doing a yoga routine; and you can do simple strength-building exercises to build strength and tone your body.

Let me explain why this is important.

### Stamina

Stamina or endurance is the measure of your body's ability to sustain prolonged stressful effort. It provides valuable insight into your overall physical constitution and your power to

endure fatigue. Thus, by building your stamina you can ensure that your delivery process is relatively easier and stress-free.

Stamina develops when the body moves in a rhythmic and continuous manner, using the large muscle groups in the body. When you are pregnant it is advisable to do low-impact exercises like swimming, cycling or walking and avoid high-impact exercises such as skipping, running and jumping.

## Suppleness

Suppleness or flexibility is the ability to achieve a full range of movements, such as stretching and bending with ease. Being supple means that you can reach up to take an item from a high shelf or bend down to tie your shoelaces, without feeling restricted in any way.

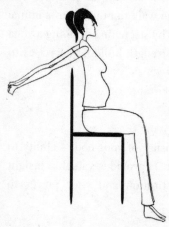

During pregnancy, because you are gaining weight, specifically in the stomach and breasts, your posture is compromised. Your back hurts and your body feels tight and stiff. Simple stretching exercises and yoga can relieve pain and stiffness. However, you should be careful while stretching, because your joints get lax due to the release of the hormone relaxin.

While stretching, a slight degree of tension should be felt in the muscles. Attempting to stretch too far may cause physical discomfort or pain and can even result in injury, especially during pregnancy. In order to improve suppleness, stretches need to be held for 10 to 30 seconds to give connective tissues enough time to lengthen.

Stretching also keeps your muscles better coordinated, helping to correct posture problems.

**The perfect stretch**
- Stretch smoothly; never bounce or jerk.
- Breathe slowly, deep and natural.
- Remain relaxed and feel the stretch.

## Strength

During pregnancy, even day-to-day activities such as sitting, getting up and lifting things require strength. When your body is strong you can get into positions easily; if not, you place undue strain on your body. Therefore, to remain fit during pregnancy, it is important to include strength exercises in your regimen. Strength training gives better balance to the body, making you less prone to injuries.

### Bare bone facts

The human skeleton comprises 206 bones.
Bones need calcium to grow and stay strong. Strength exercises improve calcium absorption in the bones and regular exercise results in increased bone density.

An effective strength routine should include exercises that target the major muscle groups of the upper body, torso and lower body. You can strength train using your own body weight, or use light weights or exercise machines.

Weight training with light weights is safe; avoid lifting heavy weights during pregnancy.

### Benefits

Upper body strengthening exercises help promote good posture. Exercises for the back and abdomen will reduce back strain, prevent *diastasis recti*, as well as strengthen your muscles for labour. Lower body exercises will strengthen the legs.

**Keeping strong**
- Use slow, controlled movements to lift weights to avoid injuring your joints.
- Work with lighter weights.
- Avoid lying on a bench to lift weights, or in any position where there is a possibility of getting hurt.

# Walking Works

'All truly great thoughts are conceived by walking.'

– Friedrich Nietzsche

If you enjoy walking alone, with a friend, or even with your dog, you already have a great routine. I believe walking is the nearest thing to a perfect exercise. It is a low-impact cardiovascular activity that works your entire body. When you walk, there is minimum strain on your joints, protecting them yet giving your heart, lungs and bones the benefit of a full aerobic workout. All you need is a good pair of athletic shoes to stride out with confidence.

Walk tall, with your head centred between your shoulders and your chest lifted. Bend your elbows and pump your arms back and forth from your shoulders. Pull your abs in and, with your feet firmly on the ground, strike first with your heel and then roll your entire foot until you push off into the next stride with the ball of your foot. The better your form, the more muscles you use.

I tell all my clients who find it hard to exercise – walking is the most convenient and natural of exercises, and it's free! Here's what some of the converts had to say:

'I love walking, but it can be a bit repetitive to do the same thing every day... so I vary my routine. I sometimes walk in the morning and sometimes in the evening, taking different routes. Sometimes my mom-in-law accompanies me, so I ease the pace. It makes an interesting change and can be quite relaxing.'

'I love walking barefoot in the garden. I recommend it to everybody! I feel one with nature as the dewy grass cushions my feet and I am lost in the beauty of the flowers and trees around...'

> **Fit fact:** When you walk barefoot in a park or garden, you feel the warm, moist sensation of the grass or the damp chill of the soil. The sense of touch on the sole is almost as highly developed as that in the hands.

## Hard walk

Don't feel like you are getting enough exercise? Up the ante! For a tougher workout, try walking on an incline. Walking on a slope increases your workload and energy requirement. The steeper the slope, the more energy you need. Always pace yourself and plan your route, so that you can tolerate the intensity and build up your stamina slowly. But you need to judge for yourself if you can handle slope walking during pregnancy. If you feel any breathlessness, exhaustion or pain, you are pushing yourself too hard.

Clients wanting to do more constantly ask me whether using weights while walking is a good thing. Absolutely not! I do *not* recommend walking with hand weights or ankle weights, because weights on the ankles, feet, wrists or hands increase the risk of injury to the knees, shoulders, muscles and tendons and could also create repetitive motion injury.

**Stretch after you walk**

Finish your walk with some simple stretches. Hold each stretch for 10 to 20 seconds.

### 1. Calf stretch

- ☞ Take a giant step forward with your right foot, keeping the right leg bent and left leg straight.
- ☞ Move your hips forward towards your bent right knee. Keep both feet pointing forward and left heel hanging on the ground. Hold.
- ☞ Change sides.

### 2. Front of the thigh

- ☞ Stand tall, hold onto a chair or wall for support.
- ☞ Grasp your right foot with your right hand. Keeping knees together, bend your right knee till the heel touches your butt. Hold.
- ☞ Repeat the same movement with the left leg.

## 3. Back of the thigh

☞ Slowly raise one leg and rest it on an elevated platform, such as a park bench or ledge.

☞ Keeping your hips square, bend at your waist and lower your trunk forward. Hold.

☞ Repeat with the other leg.

# The Strength Routine

The goal of this workout is to strengthen and tone your body. When your body is fit and strong you are better able to deal with the stress of pregnancy. Incorporate this set of 10 exercises in your workout plan to look and feel better.

**Warm up:** Start with a 5 minute warm up by walking or marching in place.

**Frequency:** 2 to 3 days a week, on alternate days.

## Home props

✓ Dumbbells or two 500 ml water bottles
✓ A mat or carpet
✓ A chair

## 1. Wall push-ups

An effective exercise that shapes the upper body.

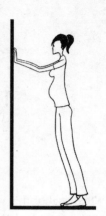

- ☞ Stand facing the wall; keep your back straight and place your palms on the wall keeping them wider than shoulder-width apart.
- ☞ Bend your elbows as you bring your chest closer towards the wall, then return to the starting position.
- ☞ Repeat for 16 counts.

## 2. Single arm row

To get the most out of this exercise, concentrate on working your back muscles. This exercise strengthens the back and improves posture.

- ☞ Place the palm of your right hand on a chair for support. Lean forward slightly so that your body is in a diagonal line.
- ☞ Hold one dumbbell in your left hand and lift the elbow upwards, pulling the dumbbell up to your waist. Gently lower the hand.
- ☞ Do 16 counts, then repeat with the other arm.

## 3. Bicep curl

This is a great exercise for creating definition and strength in the biceps. You can actually see the muscle definition when you concentrate on tensing the biceps.

- Hold dumbbells in both hands, with your palms turned outwards.
- Lift your forearms towards your shoulders, tensing the biceps as you lift, and then lower your arms.
- Repeat for 16 counts.

## 4. Overhead tricep extension

This upper arm exercise works the back of the arms. These muscles need to be strengthened as they are usually not as strong as the front of the arm.

- Sit on the edge of a chair and hold one dumbbell in both hands.
- Raise your arms overhead, and bend your elbows behind your head.
- Extend your arms back up to the starting position.
- Repeat for 16 counts.

## 5. Lateral shoulder raise

Toned shoulders help create a sculpted appearance, and make your body look more streamlined.

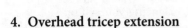
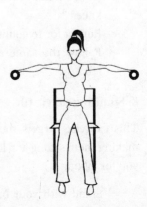

- Sit straight. Hold weights in both your hands, palms facing down and elbows bent.
- Lift your arms laterally in line with your shoulders and then lower.
- Repeat for 16 counts.

## 6. Calf raise

Persevere with this exercise, because this is one of the quickest and most effective ways to tone the calves. You will see the difference in one month.

- ☞ Stand tall, with your shoulders back and chest lifted.
- ☞ Stand on your toes and, balancing yourself on the balls of your feet, lift your heels as high as possible.
- ☞ Slowly lower your heels.
- ☞ Repeat for 16 counts.

## 7. Standing leg extension

This is an excellent exercise to strengthen the thighs.

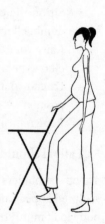

- ☞ Stand tall; use a chair to maintain your balance. Lift your right leg and bend the knee (try to bend it to a 90 degree angle).
- ☞ Now, extend your right leg from the knee.
- ☞ Repeat for 16 counts.
- ☞ Follow the same exercise with the left leg.

## 8. Standing pelvic tilt

This exercise targets the muscles of the hips, back and abs, making them strong and less prone to stress and pain, preparing you for labour.

- ☞ Stand with your back against a wall, keeping your feet

shoulder-width apart and
your heels a few inches away
from the wall.

☞ Slowly press the small of
your back against the wall,
and slide down the wall an
inch or two. Rotate your
hips so that your lower back
flattens on the wall.

☞ Hold for 10 seconds, then
release and stand-up again.

☞ Repeat for 12 to 16 counts.

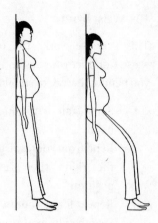

## 9. Side leg lifts

This outer thigh and hip exercise is very effective. Concentrate
on good form; be careful to avoid stress to the neck region,
especially as you lift your leg off the floor. As you come up, use
your hand to support your head; avoid tilting your chin towards
your chest.

☞ Lie on your side with your hand stretched out above your
head.

☞ Lift your outer leg slowly, slightly higher than the height
of your hips, and slowly lower.

☞ Repeat for 16 counts on each side.

## 10. Waist bends

This exercise works the obliques and the waist. Contract your abs and lower back when you bend sideways, to stabilise your pelvis.

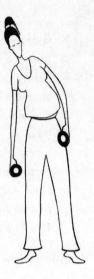

- ☞ Stand tall with dumbbells in each hand.
- ☞ Bend from your waist, leaning towards the right, then revert to upright position.
- ☞ Repeat for 16 counts.
- ☞ Switch sides and repeat for 16 counts on the left.

# The Stretching Routine

Most posture problems are a result of poor alignment, which is caused by tightness in the muscles. Stretching can help realign your body and help you maintain good posture. In fact, stretching is one of the key components of a balanced fitness programme; no workout is complete without it. It prevents injury, increases your range of movement, improves posture and keeps the body agile.

- Before stretching, it is important to warm up your muscles and joints by doing 5 minutes of light cardio exercise, like walking or cycling on a stationary bike.
- Breathe normally. Never hold your breath while stretching.
- Do not over-stretch muscles or joints to the point of pain; this can result in injury to delicate connective tissues.
- While stretching, focus on the body part being stretched.
- Use gentle, slow movements to stretch. Force or jerks can cause injury to tissues and joints.
- Stretching muscles after an intense workout can be very soothing and relaxing.
- Hold each stretch for 10 to 20 seconds.

## 1. Neck stretch

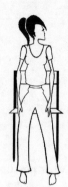

- ☞ Drop your head to the right side, bringing your ear close to your shoulder.
- ☞ Hold. Then return to the centre.
- ☞ Repeat on your left side.

## 2. Shoulder stretch

- ☞ Sit straight. Cross your right arm horizontally across your chest. Placing your left hand or forearm just above the elbow joint of the right arm, pull the right arm close to your chest.
- ☞ Switch arms.

## 3. Upper back stretch

- ☞ Clasp your hands in front of you so that you feel the stretch in your upper back.
- ☞ Lower your head during the stretch so that your chin is close to your chest. Hold.

### 4. Chest stretch

&#9758; Sit with both your arms behind
your back, clasp your hands
and slowly lift your arms, until
you feel the stretch in your
pectorals. Hold.

### 5. Overhead arm stretch

&#9758; Clasp your hands over your head,
with the palms turned towards the
ceiling.

&#9758; Pull your hands up gently and
stretch upwards; hold.

&#9758; Feel your spine and arms stretch;
breathe as you hold. Slowly release.

### 6. Shoulder rolls

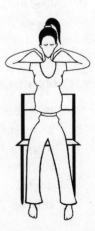

&#9758; Bend your elbows and place your
fingers on your shoulders. Roll your
shoulders 5 times in forward motion,
and then 5 times in reverse. Relax.

## 7. Waist stretch

- ☞ Stand with your feet shoulder-width apart, knees slightly bent and toes pointing straight ahead. Place your right hand on your hip while you extend your left arm over your head.
- ☞ Slowly bend at the waist to the right side and hold.
- ☞ Repeat on the other side.

## 8. Cat-camel stretch

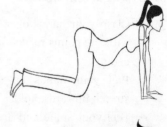

- ☞ Get down on your hands and knees. Gently arch your back and hold for 5 seconds.
- ☞ Then, gently round your back (like the hump of a camel) and hold for 5 seconds.

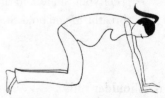

- ☞ Repeat 5 times.

## 9. Cobbler stretch

- ☞ In a seated position, bend your knees and slowly bring your feet together in a 'namaste' position. Feel the stretch in your inner thighs.
- ☞ Hold for 10 seconds.

## 10. Front of the thigh

☞ Stand tall and hold onto a chair or wall for support. Bend your right knee and grasp your foot; hold the right foot.

☞ Repeat the same movement with your left leg.

## 11. Back of the thigh

☞ Slowly raise one leg and rest it on an elevated platform, such as a park bench or ledge.

☞ Keeping your hips square, bend your waist and lower your trunk forward.

☞ Hold and then repeat with the other leg.

## 12. Calf stretch

☞ Take a giant step forward with the right foot, keeping your right leg bent and left leg straight.

☞ Move your hips forward towards your bent right knee. Keep both feet pointing forward and your left heel hanging on the ground.

☞ Hold, then change sides.

# Water Workouts
## Swimming and Aqua Aerobics

Here's some trivia for you – did you know water therapy and aqua aerobics have been around for centuries? The Greeks and Romans used hot spas and springs as therapy for different ailments. In the 1930s, US President Franklin D. Roosevelt used water therapy as treatment for polio.

The warmth and compression of the water on the muscles and joints of the body are considered very therapeutic. In fact, many doctors recommend water therapy to their patients for recovery and rehabilitation after surgeries. Thus, it is only natural that water exercises are comfortable and soothing for pregnant women as well.

I have found that swimming is extremely beneficial to pregnant women as it builds abdominal and shoulder strength – areas that are especially taxed by carrying a baby. Water exercises also reduce joint stiffness and other discomforts associated with pregnancy. Water exercise makes an ideal workout because of its low impact qualities. 'Low impact' refers to any exercise that is easier and more comfortable on the joints, particularly the ankles and knees.

'Nothing refreshes me like water! I swim regularly – at least 3 to 4 times a week. Can I continue to do so now that I'm pregnant?'

Apart from keeping you cool, one of the greatest benefits of swimming is that it uses large muscle groups in both your arms and legs and offers a low-impact cardiovascular workout that allows you to feel 'weightless' despite the extra weight you're carrying. So if you're a regular swimmer, chances are that you will be able to continue to swim for most of the nine months, without having to modify your routine too much. Just be careful not to jump or dive into the water.

In the third trimester, concentrate on the breast stroke. It is a good workout for your chest and back muscles, which are the two areas most out of alignment during pregnancy.

## Aqua aerobics

Dr Jeremy Sims (GP & public health nutritionist), in his article 'Aerobics: Water Aerobics', recommends water aerobics as not only 'a more comfortable workout, but a better workout all around'. Walking on land for 30 minutes uses 135 calories, while swimming for the same amount of time uses 264 calories due to the resistance produced by water.

Water acts like a liquid weight machine, providing resistance, cardiovascular exercise and improved range of motion. Swimming or aqua exercises are non-weight bearing exercises; they place minimal stress on the bones and joints. They tone your entire body, build stamina, strengthen your heart muscles and improve delivery of oxygen to the muscles.

**Fit fact:** When you run, every time your foot hits the pavement, a shock equivalent to five times your body weight travels up your legs and into your spine. Exercising in water minimizes this shock impact, protecting your joints. Experts believe that the buoyancy of water can reduce the impact on your joints by as much as 85 per cent.

**'Is aqua aerobics better than other workouts?'**

This is a question I am often asked. Yes, it is a wonderful exercise if you enjoy water and if you have access to a swimming pool. But it is fine if you prefer exercising on land. You need to discover your exercise personality – what are you happiest and most comfortable doing? I assess my clients' needs and fitness levels before I recommend any exercise plan. Consult your doctor/prenatal fitness instructor to figure out an exercise plan that suits you best.

**'Do I need to know swimming to take part in aqua aerobics?'**

No, you do not have to be a swimmer to take part in aqua exercises. It is easy and safe, as well as beneficial to all levels from beginner to advance. Begin by exercising in the shallow end of the pool and as you progress you may move from knee depth to chest height. Don't worry, your feet will always touch the floor. In fact, many of my clients felt that these exercises boosted their confidence in the water and improved their swimming.

Here is a simple leg strengthening exercise that you could try:

✓ Stand in the shallow end of the pool facing the steps. Step onto the lowest step, and then go back down. Repeat 10 times slowly, leading with your right leg; then 10 times leading with your left leg.

Remember these guidelines when exercising in the pool:

As with all forms of exercise during pregnancy, consult your doctor before you start.

Swim regularly for 20 minutes three times a week to get maximum benefit.

To be safe and comfortable, begin slowly and increase gradually.

Drink plenty of water. Remember, you can become overheated and dehydrated even while swimming. Keep a water bottle nearby so you can drink before, during and after your workout.

Wear proper clothing. Get yourself a stylish maternity suit that supports your breasts and belly.

If you're in an outdoor pool, be sure to wear sunscreen (SPF 15 to 30) and a cap or visor to protect your skin, which is extra-sensitive during pregnancy. Avoid swimming at the hottest times of the day (between 10 a.m. and 3 p.m.).

Do not expect to keep your pre-pregnancy pace. There are changes in your body that make balance and flexibility more complicated. Water offers a lot of resistance and trying to move your growing body through it can be very tiring. Slow your movements as required so that you are not exercising to exhaustion.

Listen to your body. If you feel any signs of fatigue or dizziness, headaches or cramping, stop immediately.

Shower immediately after your swim, since pool chemicals can irritate and dry your skin and hair.

# Prenatal Yoga

'Yoga, an ancient but perfect science, deals with the evolution of humanity. This evolution includes all aspects of one's being, from bodily health to self-realization. Yoga means union – the union of body with consciousness and consciousness with the soul. Yoga cultivates the ways of maintaining a balanced attitude in day-to-day life and endows skill in the performance of one's actions.'

– B.K.S. Iyengar

Yoga is a discipline that focuses on the balance between mind and body. Yoga combines asanas, pranayam and relaxation techniques to achieve this balance.

Yoga has become very popular because of its holistic approach to balancing and strengthening your body, mind and spirit. It can be especially beneficial for pregnant women since it encourages you to stretch, breathe and relax, which in turn can help you adjust to the physical demands of pregnancy, labour, birth and motherhood. It calms both mind and body, providing you with the physical and emotional stress relief you need throughout your pregnancy.

My client Maya had a difficult time in her first trimester. She felt tired, nauseous and low on energy. As a result, she was stressed and irritable. I started her on yoga in her second trimester. At first she found it too slow. She felt she was not doing enough. After a few weeks she began to feel the difference. Later she told me,

'Yoga was the best thing to happen to me during my pregnancy. The asanas helped relieve my stiffness and the breathing exercises calmed me down. I actually began to enjoy my pregnancy!'

When practised regularly, yoga helps improve your physical, mental and emotional well-being. It improves your blood circulation, muscle tone and flexibility. And it continues to have benefits after pregnancy too. Postnatal yoga, which can be started about six weeks after the birth, strengthens the abdominal and pelvic floor muscles, helping you get back to your pre-pregnancy shape faster.

Before you sign up for that yoga class:

✓ *Consult your doctor.* At the risk of sounding like a broken record, this important fact needs to be stressed over and over again. Before embarking on any fitness programme during pregnancy, talk to your doctor. She will be able to advise you if yoga is suitable for you or not.

✓ *Find a qualified yoga instructor* or *opt for a prenatal yoga class.* Choose an instructor who is well-qualified and experienced in teaching pregnant women.

## When do you start?

If you have been practising yoga already, you can continue during your pregnancy. However, if you are planning to start yoga as a form of exercise during pregnancy, it is ideal to do so in the second trimester. Check with your yoga instructor and doctor before starting yoga in the first trimester.

## How often?

Yoga can be performed once a week or every day. The duration can range from 5 to 60 minutes per session. An important thing to remember is that if you are a beginner, you need to ease your way into yoga. Your instructor will help you find your rhythm gradually. Avoid overdoing any movement and always listen to your body. Following a gentle approach will reap the best results over a period of time. Yoga is the integration of your mind, body and soul and you have to achieve this at your own pace.

Here are some safety guidelines to help you enjoy yoga without feeling any pain or discomfort.

✓ Listen to your body carefully. If you feel any discomfort, stop. You will probably need to modify each pose as your body changes. A qualified prenatal yoga instructor will customise your yoga routine to suit the stage of your pregnancy.

✓ Avoid lying on your back after the first trimester; it can reduce blood circulation to the uterus.

✓ Avoid poses that stretch the muscles too much. You are more at risk for strains, pulls and other injuries right now because of the pregnancy hormone relaxin, which softens and relaxes joints and connective tissue.

✓ From the second trimester – when your centre of gravity starts to shift – do all standing poses with your heel against the wall or use a chair for support, to avoid losing your balance and risking injury to yourself or your baby.

✓ While twisting, move from the shoulders and back, rather than the waist, to avoid putting pressure on your abdomen. Twist only as far as it feels comfortable – deep twists are not advisable in pregnancy.

## The yoga routine

Yoga is a great way to keep your body supple and fit during pregnancy. Yoga asanas invigorate the body and mind, stretch the spine and allow better energy flow.

**Yoga tips**

- Yoga can be practised anywhere – indoors or outdoors. Just make sure it is a calm and quiet environment with adequate ventilation.
- Yoga gear should be comfortable, convenient and simple. All you need is loose, comfortable clothing and a yoga mat, rug, blanket or carpet.
- Hold each yoga pose for 10 to 60 seconds.
- Set aside a fixed time for yoga.
- If you have never tried yoga before, first learn the different poses under supervision. Start slowly and relax for 2 to 3 minutes after every asana if required.
- Yoga can be performed once a week or every day. The duration can range from 5 minutes to 60 minutes per session.
- Never force your body into a stretch or pose. Regular practice will make seemingly impossible poses more accessible.
- If you feel any pain or nausea, stop and contact your doctor immediately.

## 1. Palm tree

Imagine you are a palm tree swaying in the wind.

*Benefit:* This pose stretches and strengthens the torso

- ☞ Stand upright, raise your arms overhead and interlock your fingers.
- ☞ Now stretch slowly and gently to the right and then the left, imitating the swaying movement of a palm tree.

## 2. Modified triangle pose

Can you position your body in such a way that it forms three triangles?

*Benefit:* This pose regulates the digestive system and massages internal organs like the liver.

- ☞ Stand with your feet wide apart and arms extended at shoulder level parallel to the floor.
- ☞ Stretch your left hand overhead and bend down to the right side and touch your knee. Look up at your left hand.
- ☞ Return to starting position and switch sides.

### 3. Modified forward bend

Reach forward with your hands, with a chair for support.

*Benefit:* This pose stretches the back and legs.

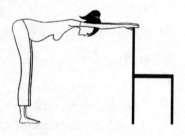

- ☞ Stand tall in front of a chair.
- ☞ Lift your arms and reach towards the chair; press your palms on the chair. Keep your back straight and bend from your hips. Hold.
- ☞ Return to standing position.

### 4. Seated twist

Twist to the right and then to the left, to improve the mobility of the spine.

*Benefit:* This pose stretches the spine, improves digestion and relieves constipation.

- ☞ Sit with your legs stretched out in front of you. Bend your right knee and take the right foot over the left knee.
- ☞ Bring the left arm and elbow over the right knee. Keep your right hand behind you on the floor for support. Now twist your torso to the right and turn your head back.
- ☞ Return to starting position and switch sides.

## 5. Cat-camel pose

Imitate a cat and then a camel. Arch your spine like a cat and then lift it up like the hump of a camel.

*Benefit:* releases spinal stress

- ☞ Get down on all fours on your mat. Place your hands directly below your shoulders. Now lift your tailbone up towards the ceiling so that your lower back is concave. As you do this your head will lift up naturally towards the ceiling.

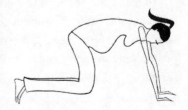

- ☞ Now round your back like the hump of a camel and roll your head towards your chest. Make the movements as fluid as possible.

## 6. Butterfly pose

Imitate a butterfly.

*Benefit:* Increases mobility of the hip joints and stretches the inner thigh.

☞ Sit with your legs outstretched on the mat. Bend your knees and bring your feet in as close as possible, towards you. Bring the soles of your feet together.

☞ Keep your spine straight and gently move your legs down and up, resembling the movement of a butterfly as it flaps its wings.

## 7. The modified corpse

You need to relax in order to feel rejuvenated.

☞ Lie on your left side; place a pillow between your legs and below your head for support.

☞ Close your eyes and relax your mind.

To make the poses more comfortable, use blankets, pillows, cushions and chairs for support if you need them. For instance, you can perform seated positions on a folded blanket. If maintaining an erect spine is difficult, lean against a wall for support.

# Relaxation and Breathing

Pregnancy has been compared to running a marathon. You are overworked, overstressed and fatigued, and the finish line seems really far away. Make it a habit to spend 10 to 15 minutes a day in total relaxation. During the third trimester, longer periods of rest and relaxation may be required.

Here are some of my favourite relaxation techniques to help you through the pregnancy. These can be most effectively performed in a comfortable sitting or lying position with your eyes closed. The relaxation space should be dimly lit, quiet and free from distraction.

## Tension/relaxation

**Aim:** To learn the difference in muscle tension and relaxation and to be able to relax when desired. Relaxing the body helps the mind to relax as well.

**Position:** Lie on your back with a pillow under your head and knees. Rest your arms at your sides and keep your legs extended and apart. After the first trimester, lie on your left side and bend the right knee. Place a pillow under the right leg.

**Exercise:**

1. Close your eyes and breathe normally.
2. Tighten the muscles of each body part in the progression listed below, and then completely relax the individual body part. Recognize the difference in feeling between a tensed body part and a relaxed one.
3. Make a fist and tighten your hands, and then relax.
4. Bend your elbow, keeping the palm open, and make a fist, tightening the arm and forearm; then relax.
5. Shrug your shoulders to the ears, tighten shoulders and then relax.
6. Flex the ankle and tighten the thigh muscles and then relax.
7. Tighten the buttocks together and then relax.
8. Tense your head and neck and then relax.
9. Make a face, tightening the jaw, eyes, forehead and mouth, and then relax.
10. End this session with five rounds of deep breathing. Inhale and exhale slowly and deeply – five times. Every time you exhale, say to yourself, 'I am completely calm.'

## Abdominal/diaphragmatic breathing

**Aim:** Abdominal or diaphragmatic breathing can help you relax during the first and second trimester (during the third trimester, due to increase in abdominal size, this exercise may be difficult to perform). As the abdominal wall relaxes and keeps rising, there is less pressure against the contracting uterus. If done slowly, one breath will last through the contraction.

**Position:** Sit on a chair.

**Exercise:**

1. Place your hands gently on your stomach and relax your whole body.

2. Slowly breathe in and out, feeling your stomach expand or rise as you inhale. The stomach should rise on each inhalation and fall on each exhalation.

3. Breathe as slowly as possible, making each breath last longer than the preceding one. Do not allow the chest or shoulders to rise.

4. Practise this abdominal or diaphragmatic breathing for 3 to 4 minutes per day.

## Imagery

**Aim**: Visualizing images helps take the mind off anxieties and unwanted tension.

**Position:** Lie on your side with your knees bent and a pillow under your head.

**Exercise:**
Try and imagine you are in your favourite place:

   Walking along the beach at sunset
   Floating on a raft in the swimming pool on a sunny day
   Sinking your head into a soft pillow

Visualize the place in detail.

# Stress Busters

There are only
two times
I feel stress:

DAY and NIGHT

Pregnancy is a happy and exciting time, but it can also be stressful. Any major change in your life can create anxiety, and having a baby certainly changes your life!

Most women undergo a mixed bag of emotions during pregnancy. My client Payal recalls, 'I was a physical and emotional wreck when I was pregnant! I was apprehensive about undergoing labour and delivery. My body would tense and I often got a headache. I realized I needed to help myself, so I started going to the spa to get facials and head massages. I also attended yoga and breathing classes thrice a week. This really helped me relax and I was better able to cope with the stresses of pregnancy.'

Did you know that emotional tension and muscular tension are linked? Research indicates that if you are tense, your muscles become tense too. This can lead to headaches and joint and muscle strain.

Here are some instant de-stressing solutions to help you chill:

### Deep breathing

Close your eyes and take seven slow, calming breaths. Every time you inhale, focus on breathing in the calm and as you exhale, breathe out the mental tension.

### Palming

Sit cross-legged on a mat or sit on a chair. Warm your palms by rubbing lightly together. Then gently place your palms over your eyes in a cupped manner. Hold the position. Try to be as mentally relaxed as possible. After five minutes, slowly open your eyes.

Repeat this exercise several times a day.

### Tense-relax

Close your eyes and tense your entire body. Hold the tension for two seconds and then relax completely. While you relax, breathe in and breathe out in a slow, relaxed manner. Repeat 2 to 3 times.

### Exercise, exercise, exercise!

Get moving, never mind how you do it! Try yoga, walking or swimming.

Physical activity is a super stress buster. Exercise gets the blood flowing to your brain, creating an effect similar to prescription drugs for depression. Exercise also triggers the release of endorphins – the 'feel-good' hormones that produce a sense of well-being.

My Seven Commandments to bail you out of the stress trap:

1. **Communicate** your worries to your husband or a friend. This person might have a different take on the matter, one that doesn't portend the end of the world!

2. **Share** your responsibilities. This is not the time to be Supermom! Doing it all by yourself will certainly get you all the credit but also all the stress.

3. **Prioritise** areas that are important to you and focus on accomplishing those first.

4. **Say no!** No is a useful word. Think how much simpler your life would life be if you stopped taking on too many tasks by just saying No.

5. **Relax** from time to time. Learn to switch off, just like you do with your cell phone. Pursue a hobby to take your mind off your worries.

6. **Know** that not all things will be in your control. There is no reason why they should be. A little unpredictability never caused anyone any harm.

7. **Sleep** can be quite rejuvenating.

This simple strategy would help you beat stress before it beats you: maintain a **Stress Diary**. For each day of the week note down the stress-inducers for that day; the negative reactions it produced in you and the positive actions you could have taken. Maintain this diary until, reacting positively becomes a habit. Here is a sampler:

**Day: Monday**

**Goal:** To handle stress in a positive manner

**8.25 a.m.**
Situation: Stuck in traffic.
Negative response: Shouted at other drivers for being too slow.
Positive action: Did deep breathing exercises to stay calm.

**9.00 a.m.**
Situation: Missed the train.
Negative response: Ate two packets of chips waiting for the next train to arrive.
Positive action: Ate an apple and drank a glass of fresh orange juice to get energised for the day.

**12.30 p.m.**
Situation: Received an unpleasant phone call from a relative.
Negative response: Moaned to family.
Positive action: Went for a walk to the nearby park to get some exercise and a breath of fresh air.

**6 p.m.**
Situation: Needed clothes to be stitched. Tailor didn't show up.
Negative response: Cursed the tailor. Drank four cups of coffee and went around grumbling about the tailor's irresponsibility.
Positive action: Retail therapy! Went shopping for maternity clothes.

My advice: don't try to be everything to everybody. Prioritise areas that are important to you, such as looking after your health and well-being during your pregnancy. Simplify life wherever possible. If you are taking on too much, slow down. One of the best ways to de-stress is to talk things through and ask for help when you need it.

# PREGNANCY BLUES

The most important thing in illness is
never to lose heart.

— Nikolai Lenin

# Common Concerns during Pregnancy

*I expected some physical discomfort,*
*but this is ridiculous.*

'I have become extremely moody... I'm happy one moment and inconsolable the next. I feel fat and swollen. I have aches and pains all over my body. Some days I just don't feel like getting out of bed. I often find myself questioning whether this is worth it.'

It is worth every minute of it!

In the words of Jennifer Lopez, 'Pregnancy is one of the most magical times in our life... but it can also be gross.'

Most of the pregnant women I have met have suffered some, if not all these symptoms at some stage of their pregnancy. If you are among the lucky few who have felt none of the grossness, sit back and enjoy your 'magical' journey. For the rest of you in the same boat as Jennifer Lopez, rest assured, this is normal and this too shall pass.

During pregnancy your physiological processes go through significant changes and you may feel a gamut of emotions and symptoms. Believe me, none of these aches and discomforts is designed to make you miserable. They are simply side effects of the preparations your body is making for that momentous moment when your baby is born.

When you finally cradle your little bundle of joy in your arms, these trying times will be a distant memory. In fact, in a couple of years you may want to do it all over again.

This part of the book is devoted to dealing with common concerns during pregnancy and the numerous questions I have been asked time and again. I am going to address each concern and suggest remedies and relief measures arrived at after considerable research and much trial and error, to get you the relief you so crave. Take heart in the fact that through the haze of discomfort there is a finish line, even if is it barely visible at times.

## Morning sickness

Morning sickness is certainly the most visible sign of early pregnancy, so much so that I am often asked: 'I haven't had any morning sickness, am I just plain lucky or is it something I need to worry about?' Studies show that 25 per cent of all pregnant women experience no nausea and vomiting. So if you are among the lucky few, don't be alarmed, sit back and enjoy the ride. You have one less uncomfortable symptom to worry about. For the rest of you, know that almost three out of four women experience nausea during the first trimester, and half of them will be sick enough to vomit.

The nausea usually begins in the fifth week of gestation, peaks at 11 weeks and typically subsides by the sixteenth week. However, for a small percentage it can last the entire 40 weeks.

*Morning, noon and night sickness*

**'Why is it called morning sickness when I'm vomiting all day?'**

That's right, it is a misnomer. It should really be called 'anytime sickness', since it can strike at morning, noon or night. According to various theories, the causes of morning sickness include hormonal changes, relaxation of muscle tissue in the digestive tract which makes you want to throw up the food you eat, and a heightened sense of smell which all pregnant women have.

The degree of suffering varies. Not all pregnant women experience the same symptoms. It could be due to:

✓ *Tiredness:* Physical or mental exhaustion can worsen the symptoms of morning sickness.
✓ *Sickness:* If you are prone to getting carsick or seasick, you are more likely to have severe nausea and vomiting.

✓    Hormone imbalances, which differ in different women.
✓    *Stress:* Mental stress can trigger nausea.

According to some sources, nausea and vomiting in pregnancy could have a positive effect on you and your baby. Scientists suggest that morning sickness provides 'a protective mechanism for the early embryo'. Sensitivity to food like poultry, caffeine and fish may keep you from ingesting substances that could potentially harm your unborn baby.

What we do know is that mothers with nausea eat less in the first trimester and hence gain less weight (usually gaining only 1 kg). As the nausea subsides in the second and third trimesters, mothers increase their food intake and their babies catch up on their required nourishment.

**'I'm sick of being sick all the time. Please suggest a cure.'**

Unfortunately, there is no sure cure for your queasiness but here are some ways to minimize the misery of morning sickness:

✓    *Vitamins:* Take a prenatal vitamin supplement to compensate for the nutrients you may be losing, and take it at a time of day when you are least likely to throw it up.
✓    *Spice it up:* Everything your grandma told you about ginger is true! Ginger has been used for centuries to aid digestion and improve circulation.

      The easiest way to consume ginger is to make ginger tea – add half a teaspoon of freshly grated ginger to two cups of hot water. You may sweeten the tea with honey if you like, and sip through the day. Use ginger in cooking – add ginger to soup and dal, make ginger chutney, nibble on ginger biscuits, suck on ginger candy. Even the smell of ginger is known to quell the queasies.
✓    *Lemons:* Many women find the smell and taste of lemons

comforting. You could try sucking a slice of lemon or sour candy for relief.

✓ *Aromatic herbs:* These have traditionally been used to stimulate digestion – peppermint, chamomile and cinnamon teas can sometimes soothe an upset stomach. You could also suck on a clove bud or chew cardamom.

✓ *Find ways to relax:* Apart from hormonal changes, nausea can be related to stress and anxiety. Deep breathing and relaxation techniques such as listening to soothing music can help calm the mind and reduce stress.

✓ *Acupressure:* A number of studies have suggested that stimulation of the acupuncture point Pericardium 6 (P6) has an anti-nausea effect. This point, known as the neiguan, is located two finger-widths above the crease of your palm.

✓ *Eat as soon as you wake up:* Nausea is most likely to strike an empty stomach, due to the increase of acid secretion. Keep dry crackers next to your bed so that you don't have to get up for them if you wake up at night feeling hungry.

✓ *Eat at regular intervals:* One of the best ways to fight nausea is to avoid skipping meals. Keep a stash of light snacks such as fresh and dry fruit, biscuits and crackers (Marie biscuits or wheat crackers are light and easily digested), granola bars and roasted savouries with you at all times.

**Fit tip:** A combination of protein and complex carbohydrates can help combat queasiness, such as a sandwich with sprouts or chicken.

✓ *Stay hydrated:* If you're losing a lot of fluids through vomiting, it is more important to get your liquid intake right now than to get enough solids. If you find it easier to retain liquids, drink your vitamins and minerals in smoothies, soups and juices.

If it's easier to keep down solids, eat foods with high water content, for example, vegetables and fresh fruit like cucumber, tomato, watermelon and orange.

✓ *Enjoy a variety of foods:* Try switching foods often. Sick of oranges? Eat sweet lime. Experiment with hot and cold. Most women find cold fluids like chilled lemonade easier to get down. Others might prefer a frothy hot chocolate.

The bottom line is, do whatever works best for you. If it makes you uncomfortable or queasy, avoid it.

**'I used to love perfume, I never left home without it. Now it makes me sick to my stomach.'**

Smells can trigger nausea. Thanks to a heightened sense of smell, pregnant women often find once alluring aromas suddenly offensive. Trust your instinct. Stay away from smells that trigger nausea.

Wash your mouth often. Use toothpaste that you are comfortable with and rinse your mouth, especially after a bout of vomiting.

> **Excessive nausea**
> About 1 per cent of the time vomiting gets so severe that it becomes a danger to mother and baby. This condition is called Hyperemesis gravidarum and requires treatment with medication and/or hospitalization. Consult your doctor if you think this could be you.

## Loss of bladder control

**'I wet myself every time I laugh or sneeze. I seem to have lost control of my body. What is happening?'**

You are experiencing urinary incontinence – or loss of bladder control – another by-product of being pregnant. Often a little pee leaks out when you cough, sneeze or even laugh, as a result of the mounting pressure of your growing uterus on your bladder.

It is also the stress of pregnancy and delivery that may cause the pelvic muscles to function poorly, resulting in a weakened bladder. Hence you feel the need to urinate more frequently.

Some women also experience urge incontinence, the sudden and overwhelming need to answer nature's call right away. These signs of stress incontinence and urge incontinence start early in pregnancy and the symptoms increase as the pregnancy progresses. Maintaining the strength and integrity of pelvic muscles during pregnancy and after delivery is extremely important and can help prevent further urinary stress incontinence. A strong, coordinated pelvic floor will improve bladder control and assist in the second stage of labour – the pushing phase.

To improve your pelvic floor function and muscle strength, perform these simple exercises:

## Kegels

Named after their inventor Dr Arthur Kegel, kegels are considered the 'wonder exercise of pregnancy'. They help strengthen and protect the muscles of the pelvic floor and are a requisite of any pre- or post-natal exercise routine. Kegel exercises target your pelvic floor muscles, strengthen your urethra, bladder, uterus and rectum. I recommend kegels to all my clients – pregnant or otherwise. In fact, girls can practise kegels from the age of 15! It requires very little effort and the benefits are immense.

✓   Strong pelvic floor muscles make childbirth, specifically pushing during delivery, much easier.
✓   It reduces the risk of 'tearing' during labour.
✓   It prevents incontinence later in life.
✓   It reduces your chances of haemorrhoids by improving circulation in the rectal area.
✓   It tones the stretched out vaginal muscles, making sex more enjoyable.

The promise of easy childbirth and better sex! Who could ask for more? So let's get started.

✓   Contract your muscles as if you're trying to stop the flow of urine.
✓   Hold this contraction for a count of three.
✓   Slowly release and relax.

Congratulations, you have just done your first kegel. It's that simple. Try to do this several times through the day, in three or four sets of 25 contractions each. As your pelvic floor muscles get stronger, increase the length of time you hold the contraction, going up to 10 seconds.

To make your workout more effective, try changing your contractions. Do some quickly, like little flutters, and the others more slowly.

### Anywhere! Anytime!

The best part about kegels is that you can do them anytime, anywhere – while watching TV, standing in line at the grocery store, sitting at your desk or driving your car. I advise my clients to make kegels a regular part of their fitness routine for life.

Here are my tips to help control stress or urge incontinence.

✓ Empty your bladder as completely as possible every time you pee.
✓ Practise your kegel exercises diligently.
✓ When you feel like coughing, sneezing or laughing, cross your legs or do kegels.
✓ Wear a pantyliner to avoid an embarrassing incident.
✓ Urinate whenever you feel the urge. Do not attempt to control the urge when you feel a sensation, even if it means making frequent trips to the loo.

**Fit tip:** Continue to drink at least 8 to 12 glasses of water a day. Restricting water intake leads to dehydration and may even result in urinary tract infection.

## Constipation

Feeling stuffed, gassy and heavy? Feel like you can't go to the loo properly? Chances are you are constipated, a common problem in pregnancy, affecting at least half of all pregnant women.

Constipation can start as early as conception and persist right through your pregnancy. It is caused by the pressure of your growing uterus on your rectum, along with high levels of the hormone progesterone, which slows down the passage of food through your digestive system. This causes the muscles of the bowel to relax, making them sluggish. Furthermore, the iron supplement that you need to combat anaemia has a constipating effect.

You are more susceptible to constipation if you had this condition in your pre-pregnancy days and if you lead a stressful or sedentary lifestyle.

Constipation can be a tough condition to deal with, but deal with it you must. I recommend these tried and tested ways to combat constipation and alleviate your symptoms:

### Eat fibre

Fibre adds bulk to food and is an important source of roughage. The roughage component in fibre, which is also referred to as 'nature's broom', aids the digestive system, helping the body's elimination process.

The National Cancer Institute of America recommends a daily intake of between 20 to 35 grams of fibre-rich foods. Dietary fibre is found in fruits, vegetables, sprouts, beans, legumes, flax, wholegrain cereals, nuts and seeds.

### Drink water

Water regulates the body temperature, assists the digestive system, carries nutrients and eliminates waste from the body. On an average you need to consume 8 to 12 glasses of water every day.

### Avoid large meals

Big meals are hard to digest and can make you feel sleepy. When you consume 6 to 8 small, healthy meals every day, your body needs more calories to break down the food, thereby helping to increase your body metabolism.

### Sit down and eat slowly

It is easy to overeat when meals are grabbed on the run or while standing in front of the refrigerator. Eat slowly, to give your body time to release the enzymes that tell your brain you have had enough.

### Try reflexology

Try a simple reflexology treatment at home. Ask your partner or a friend to massage the arches of your feet (these are the parts which correspond to the foot reflexology zones for the digestive system) in a circular, clockwise motion, for about five minutes on each foot.

### Watch the clock

The later you eat, the harder it is to digest the food. If you must have a late dinner, eat a small snack in advance; this way you won't be ravenous at dinner time. Give yourself two or three hours to digest any meal before going to bed.

### Don't overeat if you are stressed

Avoid eating as an antidote to emotional pain. Consumption in excess of what you need can lead to digestion problems and weight gain.

### Eat healthy

Choose fresh, organic foods rather than refined, processed foods that are full of additives.

*Exercise regularly*

An active body = active bowel movements.

Remember this: Exercise! Exercise! Exercise!

Walking, swimming, cycling on a stationary bike and yoga all help ease constipation and leave you feeling more fit and healthy.

**Fit tip:** Follow an exercise routine from my exercise section that is appropriate to your fitness level. Don't overdo it - listen to your body.

## Super foods that assist digestion

*Mint*

Mint tea is used as a treatment for indigestion, colic, heartburn and flatulence. It can also stimulate the appetite and cure nausea and headaches.

*Figs, prunes and raisins*

These improve digestion and elimination. Rich in iron and calcium, they also improve blood quality and build strong bones.

**Fit tip:** Soak figs, prunes or raisins in warm water for 10 to 15 minutes before consuming, to make them easier to digest.

### 'When is constipation serious?'

For most women it's more an inconvenience than a major problem, but if it persists, you should consult your doctor. Sometimes constipation can lead to haemorrhoids or piles, which can be extremely uncomfortable, but is treatable. Rest assured, both conditions should resolve themselves fairly soon after your baby is born.

## Haemorrhoids or piles

Haemorrhoids are varicose veins that appear just inside or outside the anal opening. These swollen enlarged vessels lie under the surface of the skin and can lead to irritation of the skin and, occasionally, bleeding with bowel movements.

The good news is, haemorrhoids aren't dangerous, just uncomfortable, and they usually go away after delivery. But in some cases, they can develop post delivery as a result of pushing during delivery.

Here are some tips to help prevent or reduce problems from haemorrhoids:

✓ Avoid getting constipated. Try not to push or strain yourself when you are having a bowel movement.

✓ Keep your feet elevated on a stool to enable easier bowel movement.

✓ Do your kegels regularly. It can ward off haemorrhoids by improving circulation in the area.

✓ Avoid standing or sitting for long hours.

✓ Use a doughnut-shaped pillow to ease pressure on your bottom.

✓ Sleep on your side instead of your back, to take the pressure off.

✓ To soothe the inflammation, fill your bathtub with warm water and sit in it. The warm water can help clean the area if it is too painful to wipe.

*Please note:* Consult your doctor before using any topical therapy or medication.

## Mood swings

There is a reason they are called mood swings – like swings in the playground they can swing to exhilarating highs and down to depressing lows.

**'I feel on top of the world one moment and very sad and low the next. It's like I'm on an emotional rollercoaster. Is this normal?'**

Mood swings are common during pregnancy, because of hormonal changes that affect your neurotransmitters and the wide range of feelings you may have about becoming a parent. In my experience, everyone responds differently to these changes. Some mothers experience heightened 'good' and 'bad' emotions, others feel a little depressed or apprehensive. In most cases, moodiness flares up around the first trimester, diminishes in the second trimester, and reappears in the last few weeks of pregnancy.

I remind my clients that pregnancy is probably *the* most stressful and overwhelming time of their lives. You may be overjoyed at the thought of having a baby one day and panic at the prospect the next. Even if your baby is very much wanted, it is perfectly normal to have mixed feelings about the pregnancy and what lies ahead. For instance, you may be worried about whether you will make a good mother, whether the baby will be healthy and how it will affect your relationship with your husband/partner. It's not surprising, considering expectations are so high these days, that the pressure starts long before the baby is born.

At the same time, you have to cope with your changing body; you may be grappling with the feeling that you are unattractive in your own or your partner's eyes. You may be worried about putting on too much weight or looking fat as your body expands to accommodate your baby. Add to this the physical symptoms of pregnancy, such as morning sickness, heartburn, fatigue and the many aches and pains, and life becomes one big burden. You probably feel like you've lost control over your body and your life. It's no wonder that your emotions are all over the place at this time.

So the burning question is this: 'How do I manage my mood swings?'

Reminding yourself that emotional ups and downs are normal right now and making a conscious effort to take care of yourself helps keep the blues away.

### It's time for 'I, Me, Myself!'

Sounds selfish? It's NOT! This may be the last time in your life that you can put yourself first without feeling guilty. I insist my clients take the time to do the things that make them feel good – curling up with a book, taking a nap, soaking in a warm aromatic bath, getting a prenatal massage or watching a movie with a friend. Taking the time to do something just for you is sometimes the best pick-me-up.

### Easy does it

*At home:* Resist the urge to do your chores at your usual pace. Take it easy. This is just as important as taking care of the baby inside you.

*At work:* Don't even think of taking on extra work now, especially in the first few months of pregnancy. If you think your mood swings are difficult to cope with at home, imagine what it will be like at the office. I like my client Sonia's way of dealing with her erratic moods. She put up a poster at her desk that said: 'I'm not bitchy, I'm pregnant. Next mood swing: five minutes!'

And it worked! Her colleagues gave her a wide berth and stopped bothering her unnecessarily.

**'Is food a contributing factor to my mood swings?'**

It can be. Follow these basic guidelines to better control the extreme highs and lows:

*Eat at regular intervals:* Erratic meal timings can result in fluctuations in blood sugar levels. Eat small, nutritious meals, 6 to 8 times a day, for sustained mood highs.

*Avoid a sugar rush:* Limit your consumption of simple sugar and caffeine. Chocolate, candy, soft drinks, tea and coffee will give your blood sugar a quick spike but bring you down just as fast.

*Eat well:* Remember, eating well will make you feel better physically and emotionally. Follow my pregnancy diet as closely as you can. This could help in moderating your mood and providing the all important nourishment for your baby's brain development.

'I'm irritable all the time. I find myself flying off the handle at the slightest provocation, venting all my frustration at my husband.'

It is quite normal to turn on our nearest and dearest when we are frustrated. Perhaps you feel your husband should understand, since it is he who got you into this situation in the first place! Use this time to create a special bond with him.

*Share your concerns:* Pour out your feelings to him and let him express his own. He is probably feeling the same anxiety and insecurities as you are. Just putting your concerns into words often helps dissipate them. Spend quality time together and nurture your relationship. Go on a holiday or take off for the weekend if you can. Establishing a strong connection now will reap benefits after the baby comes.

If you're single, nurture your relationship with your friends and family. It'll give you the vital support you need, now and after your baby is born. Sometimes sharing your concerns may also give you the answers you seek.

*Make love not war!* The old adage is true, especially now. Resist the urge to pick a fight, get close instead. Intimacy, such as cuddling in bed, even holding hands while watching your favourite programme on TV, can help boost your mood and put a smile on your face.

*Join a support group or an exercise class:* Most of my clients feel that their prenatal fitness class is the highlight of their day. Just the act of reaching out to other moms-to-be and sharing experiences minimizes their feelings of isolation.

And they get to exercise too – expending all that negative toxic energy! Remember, exercise releases feel-good endorphins that can send your spirits soaring to great highs.

*Banish the stress:* Recognize the sources of stress in your life and change what you can. Don't let the frustration build; find ways to unwind. Get plenty of sleep, eat well, exercise, relax and enjoy your pregnancy!

I recommend these simple relaxation techniques:

✓ Close your eyes and breathe deeply. Feel your breath moving through your body from the top of your head down to your toes. Feel each breath bringing you and your baby nourishment and energy. Feel your baby cradled safely inside your womb. Feel your breath rise and fall within you and relax completely.

✓ Bond with your baby. Place your hands on your belly and send happy, loving thoughts to your unborn child.

✓ Read enchanting stories and beautiful poetry aloud to your baby.

✓ 'If music be the food of love, play on,' said Shakespeare wisely. There's nothing like listening to soothing music to calm frayed nerves.

✓ Cherish the moment. Take the time to relax, eat well, drink plenty of fluids and get regular exercise.

## Swelling

**'I'm in my seventh month and just when I thought the end is near, my legs and feet have started swelling up, making it really hard to walk.'**

Just when you think your body has been through the whole gamut of changes expected during pregnancy, a new symptom crops up in the last trimester. It is almost as if, to keep up with your swollen belly, your extremities start swelling too. You will notice your feet getting cramped and the rings on your fingers becoming tighter.

Studies indicate that 70 to 80 per cent of women develop oedema or a mild swelling of the ankles, feet and hands at some stage during their pregnancy. In rare cases swelling can be severe, making it difficult to walk.

During pregnancy your overall blood volume increases. This increases the total fluid volume circulating in the body. Some fluid escapes out of the blood vessels into the tissues, causing swelling in the area – most commonly, the hands and feet. Hot weather or a high sodium diet can make it worse. The hormonal changes that your body is going through may also result in fluid retention and the enlarging uterus places pressure on the large veins that return blood to the heart.

You will notice that the swelling increases as the day progresses, especially if you've been sitting or standing for long periods of time. But rest assured, it will dissipate if you lie down for a few hours.

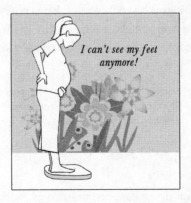

Again, like so many symptoms of pregnancy, this is temporary! It should disappear within a week or two of delivery. The fluid gets cleared from your body through your kidneys.

Aside from humour, I recommend these simple adjustments:

✓   Keep moving. Don't sit or stand for long periods. Prop your
    feet up on a stool while sitting. Take frequent walks to get
    your circulation going.

✓   Choose comfortable footwear and avoid tight-fitting
    clothes.

✓   Massage your feet, legs, arms and hands. Soak your feet in
    a tub.

✓   Limit your intake of salty foods such as potato chips, papad,
    pickle, salted nuts and canned foods.

✓   Drink lots of fluids to avoid water retention. The more water
    you drink, the more toxins you will flush out from your
    body.

✓   Keep active – exercise helps keep the swelling down.
    Walking, swimming or water aerobics are ideal because they
    place minimal stress on the joints, improve circulation and
    reduce swelling.

✓   Wear stockings. The compression helps relieve swelling.

✓   Lie on your side to reduce the pressure of the uterus on the
    veins, to increase circulation and to reduce swelling.

> If your swelling is more than mild, consult your
> gynaecologist. In rare cases, leg swelling can be
> a sign of pre-eclampsia, a condition that causes
> headaches or high blood pressure.

## Dizziness

Feeling faint or dizzy can certainly be alarming, but it is a
common concern during pregnancy. In the first three months
of pregnancy, your blood pressure is lower than normal, which
is why many women complain of dizziness in the early months.
Dizziness may occur because there is not yet an adequate blood
supply to fill your rapidly expanding circulatory system. In the

second or third trimester it is caused by the increasing pressure of your baby on your circulatory system.

**'I feel dizzy when I change positions or exert myself too much. Is something wrong?'**

*Getting up too quickly* often results in a sudden decrease in blood pressure and can cause dizziness. Make sure you stand up slowly.

*Inadequate water intake* causes dizziness – make sure you're drinking at least 8 to 12 glasses of water every day.

*Low blood sugar* might make you dizzy too. Ensure that your diet contains cereals like crackers and toast, and vegetables, fruits and other savouries, to avoid a decrease in blood sugar levels.

**'Sometimes I feel hot and dizzy when I'm out running errands... It's so embarrassing.'**

There's absolutely nothing to be embarrassed about! Everybody loves a pregnant woman. How often has a stranger smiled at you on the street or offered you their seat on the metro? Or even helped you with your groceries? I always tell my clients, this is a precious time in your life; take every precaution necessary to be safe, and enjoy the pampering.

Be mindful that overcrowded or overheated environments can cause dizziness. For immediate relief, get some fresh air and drink water. If you feel faint, try and sit down wherever you are, no matter how self-conscious it makes you feel. Some pregnant women might even lose consciousness for a few moments. This is not harmful or dangerous to the baby or to you, except if you fall and injure yourself when you faint.

Remember: stop before you drop! Never exert yourself to the point of exhaustion. Pace yourself – your body will tell you when it needs to work and when it needs its rest.

How to prevent dizzy spells

✓  Get out of bed slowly. Roll onto your left side and sit up. Remain sitting at the edge of the bed for a few minutes before you stand up.

✓  Dress cool – wear fabrics that breathe.

✓  Take a cold shower.

✓  Drink lots of fluids – 8 to 12 glasses a day.

✓  Eat regularly – 6 to 8 meals a day.

✓  Don't stand for long periods; if you must stand, walk around from time to time.

**Fit tip:** When you feel dizzy, lie down on your left, with your feet raised on a pillow or small stool to help increase circulation to the brain. Loosen any tight clothing and breathe deeply. Drink something as soon as you feel better. Contact your doctor and report this incident.

## Fatigue

Though morning sickness is the most famous sign of pregnancy, fatigue is probably the most common.

'Why do I feel so tired all the time?'

At the risk of repeating myself: this is normal, especially in the first trimester, and this too shall pass.

You're making a baby! And even though it may not be obvious externally, there is plenty of additional work taking place internally. Many consider the first few months to be the most important in a pregnancy. In fact, if you believe the old wives' tale, you should not be shouting about your pregnancy from the rooftops till you've completed your first trimester. It's not only a critical time in your pregnancy, it is potentially the riskiest.

But don't be alarmed, I'm going to explain what's going on behind the scenes.

Your body is working overtime to create placenta, a vital organ that supplies nutrients and oxygen to the baby and helps remove waste products. This organ connects your developing baby to the uterus which, over the next nine months, will nourish and carry your baby to term.

Further, the blood volume of your body increases in order to support your baby's development and there is an increase in your heart rate and metabolic rate. When your body starts adjusting to these changes, you often feel as if you're competing in a never-ending marathon.

The good news: there is a finish line. After the first trimester, once the manufacturing of the placenta is complete and your body has adjusted to the changes, you feel a little more energized and a little less tired. It is important to understand that fatigue is simply your body's way of telling you it needs rest.

Pamper yourself, especially in these first few months. Focus on taking care of yourself and get all the rest and relaxation you need. Get additional help for household chores, delegate responsibilities to your partner. If you have other children or young nieces and nephews, get them involved – you'll be surprised to see how eager they are to help you in your hour of need.

**'I get home from work exhausted, and can't wait to crawl into bed at night.'**

*Do more to do less:* I always advise my clients to adjust their schedule. For example, if you are peppier in the mornings but find yourself wilting by afternoon, see if you can schedule your toughest tasks early in the day, so that the afternoon is less hectic. Cut back your working hours or work at home, where you are more relaxed. You could even enlist the help of your co-workers to lighten your load. Most establishments look kindly at pregnant women and make allowances for them, so make the most of it.

*Power it:* Get into the habit of taking power naps at least twice a day. Even a 15 to 20 minute catnap makes a difference. If you work in an office, put your head down on your desk, and rest. My client Pooja would put two chairs together in her office and take a power nap. She says: 'These power naps really refreshed me and gave me the energy to last through the day.' She would wake up revitalized, eat a snack and get back to work.

*Eat right:* Maintain your healthy diet of vegetables, fruits, wholegrain cereals, milk and sprouts; and limit junk foods. Snack on healthy food, such as a wholegrain sandwich with cottage cheese, buttermilk and crackers, fruit and yoghurt, or an energy bar. Remember to eat 6 to 8 small meals through the day.

Cut down on caffeine; drink chamomile or decaffeinated herbal tea (check with your doctor for his advice on which teas to consume) and make sure you're drinking plenty of water to stay hydrated.

'I drag my feet during the day and look for any excuse to lie down. Where will I find the energy to exercise?'

*A little goes a long way:* Strangely enough, too much rest and not enough activity can heighten fatigue. Any moderate activity, like a short walk, can actually make you feel rejuvenated. But don't overdo it – you should feel energized, not exhausted.

*Sleep like a baby:* Try to get deep sleep. Understand your body's sleep needs. If you feel that you need more rest, increase the duration of your sleep – you should feel refreshed when you wake up in the morning.

Take heart! Remember, it won't be long. If you're in your first trimester, you will have more energy in the second. If you're nearing the end of your pregnancy, your baby will be here before you know it.

Take frequent breaks through the day to stretch and breathe deeply. I end all my exercise classes with this relaxation technique for 5 to 10 minutes. You could practise this anytime, anywhere!

✓ Close your eyes and breathe deeply; relax each body part.
✓ Infuse energy into your body with every fresh breath.
✓ Feel your breath moving through your body from the top of your head down through your neck, chest, stomach, back, hips, thighs and feet, to your toes.
✓ Imagine the tiredness reducing with every exhalation.

## Indigestion and heartburn

'Why do I feel bloated and uncomfortable after eating?'

You are experiencing indigestion, a common concern during pregnancy. The high levels of oestrogen and progesterone in your body slow down the digestive process, causing stomach discomfort, nausea, bloating and indigestion, especially after a heavy meal.

Many women complain of heartburn, a sudden burning sensation in the chest. This occurs because of the pressure of the growing baby on the stomach. The valves of the food pipe relax, allowing the stomach acid contents to flow backwards or be pushed upwards into the food pipe. These acids irritate the sensitive oesophageal lining through which food passes, causing heartburn.

Alas, there is no guaranteed way to avoid heartburn or indigestion, but here are my tips to reduce the severity of your symptoms:

✓ Eat slowly. Chew every bite thoroughly.
✓ Eat light. Reduce the quantity of food per meal.
✓ Sip warm water through the day.
✓ Sit upright after meals for at least two hours.
✓ Exercise regularly to keep the body fit and functioning efficiently.
✓ Keep your mind relaxed while eating and also for a while after your meal, as stress or anxiety can increase stomach discomfort.
✓ When you are sleeping, keep your head propped up with a few extra pillows. You can also try sleeping upright in a comfortable chair.
✓ Wear loose and comfortable clothing, especially around your waist.
✓ Reduce your intake of tea and coffee. Too much caffeine can aggravate heartburn.
✓ Avoid foods that cause stomach distress, such as papad, pickles, fried and fatty foods.

## Back pain

As your baby grows inside you, your abdomen grows too. Your centre of gravity moves forward with the extra weight around your middle and you may find yourself leaning backward for stability. This puts pressure on your lower back and is one of the many factors that can lead to back pain during pregnancy.

In addition, hormones such as relaxin and progesterone are starting to soften the joints of your pelvis, loosening it to allow easier passage for the baby at delivery.

All this throws your body off balance. To compensate, you tend to stress your back, shoulders and neck. The result – a deeply curved back and back pain.

If you are experiencing a tugging pain in your lower back, making it difficult for you to get out of bed; difficulty in sitting for long stretches; strain in carrying your child; exhaustion from doing household chores – it is only because of the changes your body is going through, so don't worry too much about it.

**'My back hurts a lot, especially when I stand. Is there anything I can do to maintain better stability and balance?'**

*Stand tall:* A perfect posture can go a long way towards easing back pain. Try to keep your centre of gravity in your spine and pelvis rather than out in your belly. Stand erect with your shoulders pulled back. Remember, slouching can precipitate or aggravate the backache.

*Kick off those heels:* Word to the fashionista: because of the extra weight you're carrying, you need to pack away those stilettos. Think flat and comfortable. You could also consider orthopedic shoe inserts designed for muscle support.

*Put up your feet:* Kick off your shoes and prop up your feet whenever you can. If your work requires you to stand for long periods of time, keep a footstool to rest one foot on while standing. Be sure to shift your legs from time to time so that the leg muscles get a chance to rest.

*Plying the pounds:* Don't gain more than the recommended amount of weight. Nine months of carrying extra weight will take its toll on your back. If you're over the suggested weight gain, make sure you get enough rest to compensate.

*Ask for help:* Avoid straining your back to reach out for any items in the closet, kitchen or anywhere else. Get someone to assist you when you need help.

*Belt it:* A pregnancy support belt gently lifts the abdomen without squeezing and encourages a more erect posture. These comfortable and fully adjustable belts are proven to be safe and can dramatically reduce or even eliminate lower back pain caused by the strains of pregnancy.

**'I work in an office and spend long hours at my computer. I sometimes have difficulty getting up from my chair.'**

*Move it:* Sitting for long periods can be as bad as sitting the wrong way. Take a break every half hour and walk around the office or do some stretches.

*Sit right:* Sitting for long hours places excessive strain on the back. Make sure your chair has a straight back. When you are seated, tuck a firm cushion in the small of your back for support. Use a footrest to elevate your feet slightly.

**'Will carrying my three-year-old put further strain on my back?'**

Yes, most definitely. Try to encourage your child to walk. If your child insists on being carried, bend your knees slightly, make sure your back is as straight as possible, hold your child close to your body and lift him slowly.

*Weightlifting:* Avoid lifting heavy objects. If you have no choice and need to lift something, steady yourself by keeping your feet shoulder-width apart; bend at the knees, keep your back straight and lift with your arms and legs, not your back. This technique of lifting minimizes back strain.

> **Fit tip:** While carrying anything heavy, divide the load into two bags and carry one bag in each hand. This load division eases the strain on the back.

**'I feel a tugging pain in my lower back every time I try to get out of bed.'**

While getting out of bed, roll over to one side and support your body with one arm, and then get up slowly.

*Sleep soundly:* A firm mattress will relieve your back pain. If you don't have a firm mattress, put a piece of hardboard under your mattress. Sleep on your side with your knees bent and place a pillow between your knees for support.

> **Fit tip:** Lying on your back puts too much pressure on your back. Placing a pillow under your knees cuts the pressure by half. Lying on your side with a pillow between your knees also reduces the pressure.

*Try a pregnancy pillow:* These popular full-body pillows are a boon to pregnant women. They provide great support for your head,

shoulders, abdomen and legs, promote healthier circulation, and can reduce head, neck and back pain. They also help soothe aching muscles and ensure proper spinal alignment. You could use it as a nursing pillow, once your baby comes.

**'I often feel exhausted by the end of the day, and my back feels strained. Are there any simple remedies to alleviate back stress?'**

*Pamper yourself:* You've earned it. Get massaged by a massage therapist at least once a week. Ask your partner or a friend to massage your back. You now have a medical excuse to indulge in a regular back rub!

*Warm up:* Take a warm bath or enjoy a pulsating shower on your back. Use a hot water bottle (wrapped in a towel to avoid burns) on your back, hips or other sore spots to relieve pain.

*Relax:* Rest and relaxation can work wonders on your back pain. Many back problems are aggravated by stress, so learn to relax.

*Relief:* Try and rest as much as possible. Apply a hot water bottle to the lower back or buttocks to alleviate the pain. Back exercises may also help with this nagging problem. Sometimes simple leg and lower back stretches, done twice daily, can give great relief.

> **Sciatica** is one kind of back pain. It is a sharp or aching pain that usually starts in the lower back or buttocks and shoots down the back of the leg to the calf or heel. A small percentage of women suffer from sciatica during pregnancy. It is caused by inflammation or the pressure of the baby on the sciatic nerve. Sometimes the function of the nerve can become impaired, resulting in weakness or pins and needles. But sciatica may not last throughout your pregnancy, so even if it has started early you could grow out of it in later trimesters.
>
> If the condition persists or gets so severe that it starts interfering with your daily routine, or if you have trouble walking, consult your doctor.

## Exercise

In approximately 50 per cent pregnant women, back pain occurs between the fourth and seventh months. Research has shown that women who exercise during pregnancy experience back pain far less than those who do not exercise.

**Caution:** Exercise can certainly help ease your back pain, but it may also aggravate it. Take care to choose an exercise routine that reduces your symptoms and provides you with the relief you crave. Always check with your physician before embarking on an exercise plan.

Here are five stretching exercises to be performed for 5 to 10 minutes daily. These will make a significant difference to the flexibility and strength of your back. Different exercises work for different people at different times during pregnancy, so see what best suits your individual needs.

## 1. The pelvic tilt – standing

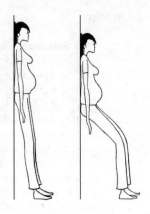

- ☞ Stand with your back against a wall, feet shoulder-width apart and your heels a few inches from the wall.
- ☞ Slide an inch or two down the wall and tilt your hips so that your lower back flattens against the wall.
- ☞ Hold the position for 5 to 10 seconds, then release and stand normally.
- ☞ Repeat for 7 counts.

## The pelvic tilt – lying down

- ☞ Lie on a mat on your back with your knees bent, tilt your pelvis by drawing the tailbone up and pressing the back down, while pulling in the abdominal muscles.
- ☞ Hold the position for 5 to 10 seconds, then release.
- ☞ Repeat for 7 counts.

The movement is minimal. Note the tightening of the abdominal muscles and the reduction in the gap between your lower back and the floor.

**Fit tip:** Practice this in your first trimester; you could feel discomfort in lying on your back in the second and third trimesters.

## 2. Cat-camel stretch

- ☞ Get down on all fours, with your hands directly under your shoulders and your knees under your hips. Your arms should be perpendicular to the floor, and not slanted.

☞ Slowly round your back, like the hump of a camel, lowering the tailbone. Then draw the tailbone up, arching your back.

☞ Repeat for 7 counts.

**Fit tip:** Keep your back flat if you have sciatica or feel any back strain.

### 3. Spinal flexion – seated

☞ Sit forward on a chair with your feet touching the ground. Move your knees apart and round your body forward, allowing your abdomen to pass between your legs.

☞ Hold for 5 to 10 seconds.

☞ Repeat for 7 counts.

### 4. Knee to chest

#### Double knee

☞ Lie on your back with your knees bent and your feet hip-width apart.

☞ Reach out to the back of your thighs and pull your knees

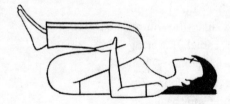

to your chest. The knees should be on either side of your belly.

☞ Repeat for 5 counts.

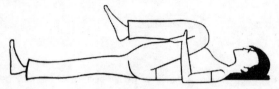

### Single knee

☞ Lie on your back, bend one knee and pull it towards the outer side of your chest.

☞ Change legs and repeat. Do this for 5 counts on each side.

### 5. Spinal rotation – seated

☞ Sit on a chair, reach one arm across your belly and grasp the opposite side of the chair.

☞ Look over your shoulder while rotating your lower and mid-back.

☞ Repeat for 3 counts on each side.

### Spinal rotation – lying down

☞ Lie on your back with your hands placed behind your head. Bend your knees and bring them close together.

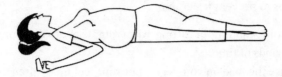

☞ Drop both legs to the right side and turn your head to look in the opposite direction. Hold for 5 seconds. Feel the lower back muscles relax and lengthen.

☞ Then, keeping your knees together, centre your legs and drop to the left side, turning your head in the opposite direction.

☞ Switch sides; repeat for 3 counts on each side.

## Leg cramps

**'I often wake up in the middle of the night screaming in pain, not from labour cramps but cramps in my legs. Is this normal?'**

Anyone who has experienced leg cramps will tell you that they can be extremely painful. These spasms of the calf muscles can attack at any time but are especially common during pregnancy. Research shows that almost 50 per cent of all pregnant women experience leg cramps, most often in the second half of pregnancy.

Why? There is no clear answer. It could be because your leg muscles are tired from carrying all that extra weight, or they may be aggravated by the pressure of your expanding uterus on the blood vessels and nerves.

Leg cramps generally start to bother you during your second trimester and could get worse as your pregnancy progresses. These painful spasms in your calves can occur during the day, but are probably more severe at night.

Tips to prevent leg cramps:

✓  Avoid standing or sitting with your legs crossed for long periods of time.
✓  Ease the load on your legs – put your feet up as often as you can.
✓  Rotate your ankles and wiggle your toes when you sit.
✓  Massage your calves and thighs with oil or cream daily. Indulge in foot massages and reflexology.
✓  Exercise or take a walk every day.
✓  Avoid getting too tired. Alternate periods of activity with periods of rest.
✓  Lie on your left to improve blood circulation to and from your legs.
✓  Drink water regularly to stay hydrated.
✓  Wear stockings or a compression bandage.
✓  Apply a warm compress to the cramped area.
✓  Avoid pointing your toes.
✓  Take a warm bath before going to bed to relax your muscles.

How to relieve cramps:

☞  Straighten your leg and slowly flex your ankles and toes, bringing them towards your nose; hold for 10 to 15 seconds. Repeat this movement 5 times.
☞  Stand at arm's length from a wall; stretch your arms forward and place your hands flat against the wall. Lean towards the wall and bend your elbows slightly. Keep your heels

firmly on the floor (you should feel your calf muscles stretching). Hold the stretch for 10 to 15 seconds. Repeat this movement 5 times.

## Pins-and-needles in your hands

Do you wake up in the night because your fingers feel like pins and needles? Do you feel sharp pains shooting from your wrist up your arm? Do you feel your hands cramping or a burning sensation in your fingers?

If you answered yes to any of these symptoms and if the pain is centred in your thumb and the first three fingers of your hand, you might have Carpal Tunnel Syndrome (CTS). More than 80 per cent pregnant women have some kind of swelling or fluid retention during pregnancy. Swelling can cause compression of the nerves. Carpal Tunnel Syndrome is the compression of the nerve in the wrist joint. This occurs most commonly during pregnancy.

If you work mainly with your hands, using repetitive motions, like typing on a computer for long hours, playing the piano, driving, writing, painting, knitting, sewing or gardening, you could aggravate this condition. Also, angling the hand back while typing or talking on the phone can worsen the symptoms.

Let me explain further: CTS places pressure on the median nerve, the nerve in the wrist that supplies feeling and movement to other parts of the hand. The area where the nerve enters the hand is called carpal tunnel. Any swelling in the tunnel can pinch the nerve, causing numbness and tingling.

But the good news is that while CTS is uncomfortable and can be painful, it is temporary and certainly not dangerous.

I am listing some simple and effective home remedies that will go a long way to alleviate your pain and discomfort.

- ✓ Adjust the height of your chair so that your work position is comfortable. When typing, make sure your wrists are straight and your elbows are higher than your hands when you type.
- ✓ Use wrist supports that keep the fingers and wrists in a comfortable position.
- ✓ Do not sleep on your hands. Place your hands on a separate pillow while sleeping.
- ✓ Wear a wrist brace while typing.
- ✓ Take frequent breaks from the computer to shake your hands and wrists.
- ✓ Use a speaker phone or hands-free if you are on the phone a lot.
- ✓ Soak your hands in ice-cold water for 10 minutes to reduce swelling.

You could also try these easy pain-relieving exercises that I recommend to my clients:

1. Keep your palm and wrist aligned and spread the fingers as far as they will go. Hold for a few secods and relax. Repeat 7 times.
2. Squeeze your hand into a fist, release and relax. Repeat 7 times.
3. Shake your hand downwards in a flicking movement.

If symptoms persist or worsen and daily tasks become difficult, consult your doctor. It is important to note that CTS is most likely a temporary condition and should disappear after delivery. In the meantime, avoid activities or exercises that put pressure on your hands and wrists.

## Abdominal separation

During pregnancy, many women experience a separation of their stomach muscles, known as *Diastasis recti*. This condition occurs when the main abdominal muscles begin to pull apart, i.e., the left and right sides of this muscle separate, leaving a gap in between.

The separated muscles do not tear or rupture; instead they thin out, creating a space in the abdomen. The condition is usually painless and causes no harm to the foetus, but it may increase back pain as a result of a decrease in abdominal support of the lower back.

Separated muscles are fairly common, and about one-third of all pregnant women experience it at some point during their pregnancy. It is more likely to occur during the second or third trimester. It may also occur during labour and delivery.

While every pregnant woman is at risk of developing this condition, the danger is greater in women who are genetically predisposed to the condition; so, if your mother or sister had it, you could develop it too. The mechanical stress of an advancing pregnancy and the hormones relaxin and progesterone also contribute to the occurrence of *Diastasis recti*.

Other factors are foetus size and number, placenta size, amount of amniotic fluid, previous pregnancy, multiple pregnancies and being overweight.

### 'How do I know if I have separated abdominal muscles?'

1. Lie on your back with your knees bent and your feet flat on the floor.
2. Slowly raise your head and shoulders off the ground, causing your abdominal muscles to tighten.

3. Place your index and middle fingers just below your belly button.
4. Press into your abdomen with your fingers. You should feel a soft gap between two hard muscles.
5. Measure the space of the gap using your fingers. If the gap is greater than two finger-widths, you may be suffering from separated muscles.

**Fit tip:** A gap of one or two fingers is considered normal. If the separation is greater than three fingers wide, you should be cautious about doing activities and exercises that directly increase stress on this area.

'Is it safe to continue my abdominal exercises at this time?'

Of course! Remember, the stronger the abdominal muscles, the more prepared you are to resist this condition. In spite of *Diastasis recti*, strong abdominal muscles help protect your back, and the stronger the abs, the easier it will be for you to push during delivery.

I have modified the abdominal exercises for a safe abs workout during pregnancy.

**Caution:** Avoid all exercises that involve twisting movements and spinal rotation as they exert a pull that may widen the gap.

## Abdominal curls or crunches on an incline

Perform this exercise on an inclined bench (at 45 per cent angle) to decrease the gravitational strain on the abdominal muscles.

☞ Lie on your back, place your hands behind your head and bend your knees. Pull your belly button towards your spine, and flatten your lower back against the bench.

☞ Slowly contract your
   abdominals, bringing
   your shoulder blades
   a few inches off the
   bench.

☞ Exhale as you come
   up, and hold for a few
   seconds, breathing
   continuously. Slowly
   lower yourself back
   down and relax.

## Splinting

☞ Lie on your back with
   your knees bent and
   feet flat on the ground.
   Wrap a long towel
   around your stomach
   with the ends in front
   of your abdomen.

☞ Do an abdominal crunch. As you raise your shoulders and
   head off the bench, pull the ends of the towel towards
   each other.

This exercise is an effective way of providing additional
support to the abdominal muscles while performing crunches.

Abdominal compression exercises train the deeper abdominal
muscles and involve pulling the navel towards the spine, while
slowly and forcibly exhaling. They can be performed at any
time, while standing or sitting.

## Lower abdominal pain

**'I feel a sharp cramping pain in my abdomen every time I stand up from sitting. Is this normal?'**

What you are feeling is lower abdominal pain, caused by the stretching of your muscles and ligaments to support your blossoming uterus. Unfortunately, this too is a normal part of the pregnancy package.

Lower abdominal pain is technically referred to as round ligament pain. As the uterus grows, the round ligament may grow as long as 10 inches due to the increased weight of the baby. Any tugging or pulling on this ligament causes lower abdominal pain.

> The **round ligament** is a fibrous band that attaches to either side of the uterus and extends downward through the inguinal canal to the labia majora. Its function is to support the uterus within the pelvic cavity.

Certain positions can aggravate round ligament pain, such as extreme stretches over the head, twisting at the waist, sudden turns, kneeling on all fours and sitting up from a lying down position.

The pain could manifest itself in a variety of ways – you could experience cramps, aches or shooting pains. It could be felt when you are getting up from bed or a chair or even when you sneeze. But rest assured, it is completely normal as long as it's occasional and there are no accompanying symptoms like fever or giddiness.

Here are some tips to deal with the pain:

✓ Wear an abdominal support belt. It helps reduce the pull on the ligaments, thereby reducing discomfort.

✓  Support your abdomen by gently bracing it with your hands when getting up or moving around.

✓  Avoid jerky movements or twisting at the waist. Slower and more controlled movements can help prevent round ligament pain.

✓  Rest your feet on a small stool when sitting.

✓  Switch to non-weight bearing exercises like swimming.

## The unilateral hip hike

☞  Stand with your hands on your iliac crests – the most prominent bones on the pelvis. (You can feel the iliac crest by pushing your hand on the side of your waist to feel the bone.)

☞  Your weight should be evenly distributed on both feet.

☞  Lift the weight off the painful side by lifting the iliac crest slightly.

☞  Hold the position for 5 seconds and release.

☞  Repeat with the other side for 3 to 5 counts.

## Pubic pain

**'My hips and pelvis hurt when I move. Is this normal?'**

Yes, these aches and pains are a normal sign that your pelvic girdle is preparing for childbirth. The pelvis is a circular bone that goes all around and meets in the middle and front. The small gap in between is connected by tissues and ligaments. When these ligaments, which normally keep your pelvic bone aligned, become too relaxed and stretched, the pelvic joint becomes unstable, causing you mild to severe pain. This pain is referred to as pubic pain or symphysis pubis dysfunction.

Pregnancy hormones relaxin and progesterone help the ligaments of your body loosen and become even more flexible than before, so that there is plenty of room for the baby to slip through during delivery. As the growing foetus demands more space, the pelvis accommodates by expanding, widening by about 4 to 7 mm by the third trimester.

Pubic pain generally occurs in the middle of pregnancy, though it can also come on as early as the twelfth week. While most women find that it dissipates after delivery, for some it may linger a little longer, diminished but still present.

Your symptoms may include one or more of the following:

✓ The most common symptom is tenderness or excruciating pain in the pubic area. The pain can increase when you're walking or climbing stairs.
✓ Difficulty in walking especially after sleep.
✓ Clicking in the pelvis while walking.
✓ A tendency to waddle.

**'When I wake up at night to go to the bathroom, I can't move my hips and legs at all. It feels like they are glued together.'**

This condition is called freezing, when the hip bone seems to be stuck in place and won't move. Some women say they have to wait for it to 'pop' into place before being able to walk.

I suggest these tips to help you cope:

✓ Use a pillow between your legs and under your belly when sleeping – body pillows are a great boon at this time.
✓ Keep your legs and hips parallel when moving or turning in bed.
✓ When standing, make sure your weight is evenly distributed to both legs.
✓ Sit down when you are getting dressed, especially when putting on underwear or pants. Pull the clothing over your feet and legs, and then stand up to pull it up to your waist.
✓ Minimize any activity that involves lifting or separating your legs, and limit walking if it makes you uncomfortable.
✓ When climbing the stairs, take them one step at a time.
✓ Avoid straddle movements; swing your legs together as a unit when getting out of bed or in and out of cars.
✓ Use an icepack to help soothe the inflammation in the pubic area.
✓ Move slowly without sudden movements.
✓ Consult your doctor about wearing a pelvic support belt to stabilize the ligaments.

My exercise advice:

✓ Avoid high impact exercises and lateral movements (such as raising your legs sideways) as these will further irritate the joint.
✓ Try aquatic exercises and cycling on a stationary cycle.
✓ Perform your kegels and pelvic tilts regularly. They can help strengthen the muscles of the pelvis.

*Please note:* If the pain is severe, consult your doctor.

## Varicose veins

Varicose veins, also called varicosities, are swollen veins that may bulge near the surface of the skin. These blue or purple, sometimes squiggly veins are most likely to appear on your legs.

Many women first develop varicose veins during pregnancy, and here's why. As your uterus grows, it puts pressure on the large vein on the right side of your body (the *inferior vena cava*), which in turn increases pressure on the leg veins. Also, during pregnancy, the amount of blood in your body increases, adding to the burden on your veins, which are already fighting gravity trying to return blood to your heart. In addition, your hormone levels rise, causing the walls of your blood vessels to expand.

### Are varicose veins hereditary?

Varicose veins tend to run in the family. You're more likely to get them if other members of your family have had them. But just because it's in your genes doesn't mean you have to be resigned to your fate. Follow the tips below and there is every chance that you could overcome your predisposition.

Varicose veins tend to get worse with each successive pregnancy and as you grow older. Excessive weight gain, carrying twins, and standing for long periods can make you more susceptible. Your symptoms may also vary in severity: you may experience little or no discomfort, or your legs might feel heavy and achy; your skin could itch or throb or you could feel a burning sensation. But be aware that they tend to get worse at the end of the day, especially if you've been standing for long periods.

Now for the good news: varicose veins tend to improve after you give birth, particularly if you didn't have this condition before you got pregnant. But even if they don't get better, don't be alarmed, there is a variety of effective ways to treat them.

Here are some tips to prevent or at least minimize varicose veins:

✓ Keep within the recommended weight gain for your stage of pregnancy.

✓ Elevate your feet and legs whenever possible. Use a stool to rest your legs on when you are sitting, and keep your feet elevated on a pillow while lying down.

✓ Don't cross your legs or ankles when sitting.

✓ Don't sit or stand for long periods – take frequent breaks to move around.

✓ Sleep on your left side; since the inferior vena cava is on the right side, lying on your left relieves the vein of the weight of the uterus.

✓ Avoid tight-fitting clothes and shoes as they restrict circulation, exacerbating the varicose veins.

✓ Wear compression stockings. They're tight at the ankle and get looser as they go up the leg. They help prevent swelling and may keep your varicose veins from getting worse.

### Exercise

Regular exercise prevents excessive fat build-up in your body. Exercise helps you maintain good circulation and tones your blood vessels.

✓ Try gentle walking, swimming and prenatal exercise classes.

✓ Try to spend at least 10 minutes each day with your feet elevated above your hips. For comfort, you could prop your legs up against a wall, bed or sofa.

## When do varicose veins become serious?

Varicose veins may itch or hurt and can be unsightly, but they are generally harmless. So if you require treatment, you can safely wait until after your baby is born.

A small percentage of people who have varicose veins develop small blood clots near the skin's surface, a condition called superficial venous thrombosis. The vein feels hard and rope-like and the area around it may become red, hot, tender and/or painful. Usually these clots aren't serious, but be sure to consult your doctor. Signs to watch out for: swelling or sores around the clot, chills or fever, or changes in colour around the veins.

> Tiny blood vessels called **spider veins** can appear near the surface of the skin, especially on your ankles, legs or face. These are called spider veins because they often appear in a web or tree-like pattern with little branches radiating from the centre. These are harmless and typically disappear after delivery.

# WELL-BEING

Health is a state of complete physical, mental
and social well-being, and not merely
the absence of disease or infirmity.

– World Health Organization

# Pamper Yourself

Your body pays for the privilege of pregnancy in ways you probably never imagined. So more than anything else, it deserves pampering.

What relaxes you? Massage, soothing music, a calm environment, self-hypnosis, a hot shower or bath – think about what might help you relax and feel better. Plan for what you need and then go ahead and enjoy it.

In this chapter I will tell you how to give your overworked body the pampering it needs without compromising on safety.

## Massage

You can begin massage therapy at any point during your pregnancy – whether in the first, second or third trimester. However, many practitioners will refuse to massage a woman who is in her first trimester. No research proves a direct connection between a massage and a miscarriage. But, because most miscarriages occur during the first trimester, most women prefer to avoid getting a massage at this time. Always ensure that you get clearance from your doctor before starting massage therapy during any trimester.

✓ To be safe, pregnancy massage should use very light strokes.
✓ During all trimesters, belly massage should be avoided because it can cause injury to the foetus. Breast massage should be avoided during the latter half of pregnancy, because nipple stimulation may cause uterine contraction.
✓ Foot, shoulder and back massage with light strokes are recommended and can induce relaxation.

*Benefits:* Are you looking for some comfort from those nagging aches and pains? There's nothing quite like a massage to relieve stress of both body and mind during pregnancy. Studies indicate that massage therapy can reduce anxiety, decrease symptoms of depression, relieve muscle aches and pains, induce sleep and even make labour easier.

*Please note*: As with any therapeutic approach to pregnancy wellness, you should first consult your gynaecologist.

Find a certified prenatal massage therapist with the training and experience to address your specific pregnancy needs.

*Body position:* Many professionals consider the best position for a pregnant woman during massage to be lying on the side. Tables that provide a hole in which the uterus can fit may not be reliable and can still apply pressure to the abdomen, or allow the abdomen to dangle, causing uncomfortable stretching of the uterine ligaments.

*Be aware of sensitive pressure points:* Trained prenatal massage therapists are aware of pressure points on the ankles and wrists that gently stimulate the pelvic muscles, including the uterus, triggering contractions. Certified prenatal massage therapists are trained to avoid pressure to these areas during pregnancy.

## Body treatments, scrubs, wraps

Body scrubs are generally safe as long as they are gentle (some scrubs may be too vigorous for sensitive pregnant skin). Some herbal wraps are safe but most are off-limits because they may raise your body temperature excessively.

## Reflexology

Reflexology is a therapy in which pressure is applied scientifically to specific areas of the body – mainly the feet and hands. The idea is that this pressure allows energy to flow freely, increasing blood flow to the corresponding part of your body and stepping up the removal of toxic wastes. And it feels good too!

Reflexology is often used to soothe the aches and pains in your back and other body parts that are taking a beating from your growing middle. In fact, reflexologists claim they can give you relief from your most persistent and wide-ranging symptoms.

As with any alternative therapy, you should consult your doctor before you begin reflexology treatments and make sure that your reflexologist has been properly trained and has experience working with pregnant women. As with prenatal massage, some reflexologists prefer to work on you only after your first trimester. And there are certain cases in which reflexology is specifically not recommended.

## Hydrotherapy

Any massage treatment using water is called hydrotherapy. This method of treatment can relax and reduce discomfort during pregnancy and labour.

Hydrotherapy is particularly effective during pregnancy because the body's physiological response to water improves circulation, it eases your aching back and feet, eases the pain of labour and delivery, and generally make you happier and more comfortable.

Depending on your symptoms, there is a variety of ways to harness the power of water:

✓   Soaking in a warm bath can be extremely relaxing. Make sure the water is not too hot.

✓   During labour, spraying your face with cold water will help you concentrate and stay calm.

✓   A cold compress on your neck will help you breathe more steadily.

✓   A warm compress placed on the lower back helps your pelvic muscles relax between contractions during labour.

Some women choose to spend much of their labour immersed in water, and some even deliver their babies in water. One reason why water works so well is that floating eases pressure on your spine, helping the pelvis open up. Once you are in the tub or in a special birthing pool, you no longer need to concentrate on your posture – your body is decompressed, which minimizes the pain of contractions. Plus, if you give birth underwater, there's less stress on your perineum, even if tearing occurs.

## Aromatherapy

Scented oils are used to heal body, mind and spirit and are utilized by some practitioners during pregnancy; however, most experts advise caution since certain aromas in concentrated form may pose a risk to a pregnant woman.

Though it is safe to use perfume during pregnancy, you may be more sensitive to smell and some scents might make you nauseated, light-headed or prone to headaches. To prevent as many unnecessary symptoms as possible, try to keep a fragrance-free environment until you discover the scents that make you feel good.

**Fragrant body sprays and lotions** have become very popular during pregnancy because they are lighter and contain less alcohol than perfume.

Certain scents like peppermint, ginger, and cardamom can fight nausea. Citrus scents such as sweet orange, neroli and mandarin can help you feel refreshed and calm. Other soft scents are lavender, rose and chamomile. Look for massage lotions in these scents and it will double your pleasure.

*Precaution:* Essential oils are different from body sprays and lotions. An essential oil is a concentrated, aromatic liquid excreted from a plant. Some essential oils can be toxic when used on the skin and are not recommended during pregnancy. You should discuss the use of essential oils during pregnancy with your doctor and aromatherapist.

Massage and other spa therapies are being used more and more today as part of routine prenatal care. In fact, experts believe that along with the guidance and advice of a doctor these therapies provide an emotional and physical health supplement that actually improves pregnancy outcome and maternal health. However, you should consult your obstetrician before beginning any therapeutic practice.

## What NOT to do!

### Saunas and hot tubs: too hot to handle

My client Mitali loved soaking in her hot tub after a tiring day at the office. 'It settles my nerves and helps me relax.' When she got pregnant, her gynaecologist banned the hot tub. Studies indicate that it takes only 10 minutes of soaking in a hot tub to raise your temperature to dangerous levels.

Extremely hot environments (anything that can raise your body temperature over 100° F) are dangerous for your developing foetus, especially in the first few months of pregnancy. You should avoid anything that might potentially increase your body temperature. Soaking yourself in a hot tub or taking an extremely hot shower could harm your baby.

> A study published in the *American Journal of Epidemiology* (2003) found that women who used hot tubs or jacuzzis in early pregnancy were twice as likely to have a miscarriage as women who did not. So if you're in early pregnancy, or are trying to have a baby, avoid any exposure to hot water that can raise your body temperature to this alarming level.

**'I'm used to going into the steam or sauna room after my workout. Can I continue to do so during pregnancy?'**

When you are pregnant, you are at greater risk of water loss and lightheadedness, symptoms that may be increased by severe heat. So steam rooms and saunas are not advised during pregnancy.

**'I suffer from severe backache. I've been using a heating pad on my back for some relief – is this bad for my baby?'**

Don't be worried if you have been using a heating pad to get some relief from pregnancy aches and pains. There is no proven danger. But from now on, be sure to wrap the heating pad in a towel to reduce the heat before you apply it to your back or any other part of your body. Also ensure that the heating pad is set at the lowest setting, apply for no more than 15 minutes at a time and never use it while sleeping.

## Sleep

**'I've always slept like a baby... until now. A million thoughts race through my head. I keep arranging and rearranging my pillows but I still can't sleep. What can I do?'**

Restless sleep is almost universal during pregnancy, especially in the last trimester. Either your baby wakes you or your bladder does. Night-time blues with heartburn and cramps don't help; the anticipation of labour and your excitement or anxiety about the baby may also keep your mind churning. Getting a good night's sleep may seem impossible...

So here are some tips to get you that all important zzzz:

*Unwind by night:* Wind down intense mental activity at least one hour before your regular bedtime. Sort out your problems before you go to bed; talk to your partner, mother or a friend so that you are relaxed and stress-free when you hit the pillow.

*Find ways to wind down:* Create a routine of relaxing before sleep. Repetitive rituals can be relaxing and help you settle down to a good night's sleep. Here are some of my favourites: light reading, soaking your feet in water, turning off the television and listening to relaxing music, taking a warm bath or getting a back massage.

*Light and airy:* If your room gets stuffy, open a window or use a fan or air-conditioner to help you sleep better.

*Beds are for sleep:* Avoid curling up in bed with work; don't read stressful documents, answer emails, or do any other work-related activity.

*Get the right sleeping support:* Your mattress should be firm enough to support your curves. Use pillows to support you or just to cuddle up with. Place pillows under your belly and between your legs.

*Eat light at night:* Take time to enjoy the food and the company. Make your last big meal of the day a relaxed one, so you have time to digest it before you turn in. Remember, a restless stomach makes for restless sleep.

*Snack if you need to:* If midnight cravings wake you up at night, have a light snack before you turn in. Old favourites – a glass of warm milk, fruit or wholegrain biscuits – can be especially soothing.

*Stay active by day:* It is a universal truth – regular exercise will help you sleep better at night.

*Limit fluid consumption before sleep:* Drinking water just before sleeping can cause midnight runs to the bathroom. But remember to get your daily requirement of 8 to 12 glasses during the day. You must drink if you are thirsty but don't consume too much water before bedtime.

*Avoid caffeine or sugar before sleep:* Drinking a cup of hot chocolate or a cappuccino at bedtime can keep you buzzing when you should be sleeping. Instead, drink some herbal tea or warm milk if you need to.

*How much sleep?* Assess your sleep by quality – how you sleep – not quantity – how long you spend in bed. You are getting enough sleep if you feel rested and refreshed in the morning. In the later stages of pregnancy you will need to shift positions more frequently, so your sleep could be disturbed. You will need rest periods and naps during the day to stay well rested during pregnancy.

## Sleeping position

'I have heard that sleeping on my stomach or back is harmful for my baby. So how do I sleep?'

As your pregnancy progresses it gets harder and harder to be comfortable when you sleep. Sleeping on your stomach is not advisable nor comfortable for obvious reasons. Sleeping on your back causes the entire weight of your baby and major blood vessels to rest on your back. This pressure can increase backaches, restrict circulation and cause dizziness.

So how should you sleep? Lie on your side – preferably the left side. Place one leg over the other and put a pillow in between. This sleeping position is recommended for you and your baby, as it results in increased blood circulation and reduces chances of oedema.

But don't worry if you wake up in the middle of the night and find yourself on your back or tummy – just roll back onto your side. Use pillows to prop yourself, the more the merrier!

Another question I am often asked: Will my baby be uncomfortable in certain positions? Babies do not feel uncomfortable like we do. They are floating in a liquid environment and have ample room to stretch. So don't worry about your baby's comfort, make yourself as comfortable as possible and catch up on your sleep while you can – before your baby comes!

# Working Mummies

Many of my clients are working mothers-to-be, and I applaud them. Most women continue working during pregnancy, and it isn't easy. But if you know how to deal with your pregnancy discomforts and stay healthy, you will get the job done!

**'I love working! In fact, my job is the only thing keeping me sane during pregnancy! What are the precautions I should take to ensure that my baby is safe?'**

If you are a workaholic, you made a smart choice! Better to keep active in mind and body than to mope around the house, depressed and miserable. However, be aware that being pregnant may present challenges at the workplace. To stay on the job, understand what needs to be done and be aware of the risks.

Here are my tips to keep the pregnancy blues away while on the job:

✓ *Food and drink:* Keep a larder of your favourite healthy snacks on your desk. Munching on khakra, crackers and apples will quell the queasies as well as ward off hunger pangs. Maintain your quota of fluids even at the office. Keep a water bottle at your desk and sip through the day.

✓ *Take it easy:* Rise leisurely in the morning and eat a healthy breakfast before you leave for work. Rushing around can exacerbate nausea.

✓  *Break it up:* Get up and move around every hour. Take power naps. Spend a few minutes with the lights off, your eyes closed and your feet propped up on a stool, to recharge your batteries.

✓  *Don't overdo it:* Consider cutting back on your activities at work and at home. Heed your body's signals and know when to stop. If you work all day, get help with the household chores. Don't try to do it all after you get home – it will just make you tired and irritable.

✓  *Early to bed:* Try to get 7 to 9 hours of sleep every night so that you are refreshed and ready for work the next day. Lie on your side to enhance blood flow to your baby and to prevent swelling in your ankles and feet.

✓  *Exercise:* Keep to your fitness routine even if your working day is long. Remember, regular exercise can boost your energy levels, especially if you sit at a desk all day. Consult your doctor and find an exercise regimen that suits your work schedule. Even a walk after work or a prenatal fitness class will keep you fit during pregnancy.

**'My work schedule and timing leaves no time for exercise.'**

In a time crunch? Here are some quick-fix exercise solutions:

✓  *10-minute fix:* Walk, even if it's in the office corridor.

✓  *20-minute fix:* Walk for 15 minutes before lunch and do exercises such as kegels, light stretches and breathing exercises for a few minutes.

✓  *30-minute fix:* Walk, swim or use a stationary bike for 25 minutes; and do kegels, light stretches and breathing exercises for 5 minutes.

**'I suffer from back strain and feel fatigued, and I'm only in my third month! I need to work... What can I do to be more comfortable at work during my pregnancy?'**

As your pregnancy progresses, even everyday activities such as sitting and standing become uncomfortable. You need to make simple adjustments at your workplace to take better care of yourself. Make it a point to move around every hour to ease muscle tension and prevent fluid build-up in your legs and feet.

✓ *Sit right:* If you sit at a desk for long periods of time, make sure your chair has adjustable armrests, a firm, cushioned seat and good lower back support. Prop your feet up on a stool. Use a small pillow or cushion to provide extra support for your back to ease and prevent back pain.

✓ *Stand right:* If you stand for long stretches at a time, put one foot up on a footrest or low stool. Switch feet as needed and walk around to keep the blood circulating. Make sure your footwear is comfortable and provides good arch support.

### Stretch at your desk

It is a great idea to take short breaks at work to stretch and release stiffness and tension from your muscles. Make use of every available opportunity to stretch – stand up and stretch when you are on the phone, go to a colleague's desk instead of emailing him, or walk around while waiting for an appointment.

### Stretches

Perform these simple stretches every day at your convenience to get rid of stiffness from your body and to relax your mind.

☞ Hold each stretch for 10 to 30 seconds.

☞ Breathe normally when you hold the stretch. Do not hold your breath.

*Neck stretch:* Drop your head to the right side, bringing your ear close to your shoulder. Hold and return to the centre. Switch sides.

*Chest stretch:* Sit straight with both your hands behind your back, clasp your hands and slowly lift them upwards until you feel a stretch in your chest muscles or pectorals.

*Upper back stretch:* Clasp your hands in front of you so that you feel the stretch in your upper back. Lower your head during the stretch so that your chin is close to your chest.

*Arms stretch:* Extend both hands straight above your head, palms touching as in a namaste.

*Shoulder rolls:* Rotate your shoulders forward a few times and then reverse the direction.

# Fashion for Two

## *Pregnant and still fabulous!*

When Shakespeare said, 'clothes maketh the man', he certainly knew what he was talking about, When you look good, you feel good. Dressing well can improve your mood and self-image at a time when these may be shaky. After all, pregnancy does have a profound effect on the body. You put on weight, your hips widen and your waist... well, the less said about your waist the better! Very soon you have to let go of your fashionable wardrobe because nothing fits.

Luckily for you, this is a great time to be pregnant. There are a large number of stores today that specialize in pregnancy fashion and there are many styles to choose from. From designer wear for the ultra hip and stylish mom to basic comfort wear for the more conventional mom.

Remember, you deserve to look and feel good, and what better way to celebrate having a baby than getting a new wardrobe made especially for you? Dressing well does not necessarily mean dressing up, especially if you're throwing up and miserable. Slipping on something fitted and trendy may comfort your soul, and even your stomach.

## For the fashionista

Hollywood moms Angelina Jolie, Katie Holmes, Jessica Alba, to name a few, have taken pregnancy fashion to new heights. They have influenced pregnant women to be trendy and fashionable throughout their pregnancy. For you, this could simply mean wearing your favourite jogging suit for running errands, a kurti and salwar for a lunch out, or a little (or big) black dress for a night out. So if you want to look chic and sexy, get rid of your ill-fitting dresses, because today's maternity style is all about flaunting those curves.

## For comfort and style

Mix and match. Invest in mix-and-match pieces in breathable fabrics that can adapt to temperature changes. Avoid restrictive clothing such as tight belts, socks or stockings. Your clothes should be free-flowing and comfortable.

Buy trendy and smart T-shirts or cotton shirts that are not only comfortable but look fashionable. Some options are cotton or linen kurtas, shirts or tunics, which can be teamed up with different salwars, churidars, capris and jeans for a new look every time.

If you like wearing pants, go in for leggings which are

available at any maternity store and pair them with trendy loose-fitting shirts or tunics. Look for leggings with a waistband that cradles the belly or is wide enough to stretch over it.

## Formal wear

You don't need to spend money on high quality fabrics for just nine months. Go for cheaper but creative options. Buy salwars, kurtis, formal pants or formal skirts that make you look trendy. Choose pants and skirts made of material that stretches – this will fit your changing shape without unsightly fabric wrinkles or bumps. Get a light jacket or cardigan that can be worn over most outfits when you want to look more formal. Add finishing touches with fashionable jewelry, comfortable shoes, light makeup and well-groomed hair.

## Shopping tips

*Shopping for two!*

*Buy the basics:* Without breaking the bank, investing in a few key items of maternity wear that can be coordinated will take you a long way. To begin with, choose clothes that are designed for the entire pregnancy – these come with adjustable waistbands, straps and buckles that can be modified to suit your size. They are comfortable and still look stylish.

*Must-haves:* Well-fitted undergarments that provide support are essential to any maternity wardrobe. Buy a couple of good maternity bras. During pregnancy your breasts will swell and grow, so you need a bra made of 100 per cent cotton with wide straps and adjustable bands.

*Lounge wear:* Tracksuits or pants in lightweight stretch jersey are ideal for comfort. Kaftans and ponchos are also great for lounging around at home.

*Beg, borrow and steal:* My client Meera said, 'I would borrow my husband's boxer shorts to wear around the house when I was pregnant. The elasticized waist was ideal for me and kept me cool. I loved them so much I still wear them in bed.'

Go right ahead! Raid your husband's wardrobe. His T-shirts, sweatshirts and pyjamas are bound to be big enough and comfy. Save your own clothes for work or when you're going out.

*Shoes:* For all you Jimmy Choo fans out there, there's no need to despair. You can continue to wear designer shoes as long as they are flat or low-heeled, are well-cushioned and provide the support you need. Put away your high heels for now; as your pregnancy progresses, your feet swell up, your centre of gravity shifts and you are more likely to trip and fall. Besides, improper footwear at a time like this could lead to lower back problems. And trendy flat shoes and sandals are always in fashion.

One of my clients said, 'During my pregnancy my feet were so swollen that the only shoes I was comfortable in were my sneakers. I used to keep a pair of formal shoes at the office so I could change if needed.'

So learn to adapt – your comfort and safety are top priority now. And remember: it's only for a little while!

## Finishing touches

*Accessorise:* Beads, bangles, watches, scarves, colourful dupattas, stoles and bags – there is an accessory heaven out there! Get creative. Liven up your white kurta with a vibrant necklace and earrings. You can brighten up any wardrobe with the right accessories. And the best thing about accessories – you can dress an outfit up or down to suit both occasion and mood.

*Makeup tips: B*etween skin discolouration and swelling, your face may meet some challenges over the next nine months. Luckily you'll be able to hide them behind the right makeup. If you have dark spots, look for brands that are designed to cover hyper-pigmentation, but make sure the makeup is non-comedogenic and hypoallergenic. Apply the concealer only to the dark spots stippling the edges to blend. Then lightly blend the foundation over the area and set with powder.

Don't be too hard on yourself. Yes, your body keeps reminding you in some weird and not-so-wonderful ways that you're going to be a mother. But it is only nine months, don't let the changes get you down. Celebrate it. Love your new curves, get a new hairstyle, play up your amazing assets. As they say, 'If you've got it, flaunt it!'

# Pregnancy Woes

## Stretch marks

More than half of all mothers-to-be develop stretch marks. This is because the skin gets stretched beyond capacity during pregnancy. These marks are most commonly caused due to sudden weight gain during the nine months. But don't despair, they usually fade (though they may not disappear completely) and become more silvery over time.

Here are some tips to help prevent stretch marks:

✓ Make sure you put on weight gradually during pregnancy.
✓ Eat a well-balanced diet, stay hydrated and exercise regularly.
✓ Apply body oil or cream to keep your skin moisturized.

My client Kavita swears by vitamin E oil. 'I used to apply vitamin E oil lavishly on my belly every night. It's yucky and smelly, but it worked. I didn't have any stretch marks post baby despite putting on 20 kg!'

Kavita got lucky. But you should be aware that despite the host of creams and oils advertised that proclaim to prevent stretch marks, there are no scientific studies that show that any oil, cream or treatment truly prevents stretch marks.

## Pregnancy skin

Pregnancy impacts every part of your body from your head down to your swollen feet. So it's not surprising that your skin is also showing the effects of being pregnant. You're likely to be more sensitive to the sun too, and get sunburn more easily.

During pregnancy, due to those raging hormones, your skin may get unusually dry or oily or itchy, or you could develop that special dewy glow that mothers-to-be often have. Always consult your doctor before applying medicated creams or taking any form of self-medication.

How to deal with skin problems:

## Oily skin

Due to hormonal changes certain skins may secrete more oil, leading to skin eruptions and pimples.

*Skin tips:*
- ✓ Wash your face with a gentle face wash a few times a day.
- ✓ Avoid using greasy creams and oil-based makeup.
- ✓ Use a light moisturizer.
- ✓ Drink plenty of water.

## Dry skin

Some women find that their skin dries up and starts to itch. Heaters and air-conditioners dry out skin even further, so if you sit in a heated or air-conditioned room, apply a heavier moisturizer.

*Skin tips:*
- ✓ Apply calamine lotion to soothe the itchiness and apply moisturizer regularly.
- ✓ Use a humidifier in air-conditioned or heated rooms.

✓ Don't neglect your skin during pregnancy – it may lose some of its elasticity and fine lines could appear on your face.

## Dos and don'ts

✓ Apply sunscreen (SPF 15 or higher) before stepping out in the sun. Try to avoid going out in the sun as much as you can, and if you must go out, make a style statement – buy yourself a wide-brimmed hat. Heed this advice even when you're not pregnant to prevent pigmentation and age spots later in life.

✓ Continue taking your prenatal vitamins throughout your pregnancy as these contain essential nutrients required by your body.

✓ Eat plenty of fruits, green vegetables and high-fibre cereals and drink lots of water daily.

✓ Perfumes, colognes and other scented soaps also irritate the skin and may cause or increase skin discolouration. Use non-scented, natural products.

✓ Wash your face with a gentle face wash and avoid using harsh soaps and scrubs that may irritate the skin further. If you wear makeup, make sure it is of good quality and clean your face thoroughly before retiring at night.

It is important to remember that all skin concerns that are caused by pregnancy usually fade away over time. The fading is gradual and it may take a while before your skin is back to normal. So take the necessary precautions to look after your skin during this time.

# Travel during Pregnancy

Generally speaking, most women continue to travel and live an active lifestyle during pregnancy. It all depends on the degree of stress, your health and risk factors, your attitude and the amount of support you get from family and friends.

**'I commute for three hours to and from work daily, often in bumper-to-bumper traffic. Is this bad for me now that I'm pregnant?'**

Unfortunately for working women, commuting has become a necessary evil, so you need to do whatever it takes to make it less stressful and more comfortable.

Make your commute more pleasant with company or an iPod. And as long as you have dinner waiting when you get home, it needn't be too stressful. But as your pregnancy progresses, long periods of sitting get more difficult. Your bladder will probably demand a stop, so make a pit stop as frequently as required. And go easy on bad roads – the jumps and jerks you experience may be uncomfortable and may cause undue discomfort.

### 'Are seatbelts safe to wear during pregnancy?'

Absolutely! Seatbelts keep you safer in the event of an accident – the same rule applies when you're pregnant. Wear the lap belt below your belly and the shoulder belt across your shoulders and chest. Be sure your seat is comfortable, keep a cushion for back support, strap yourself in and get on your way!

### 'I need a break! What is the best time to travel when I'm pregnant?'

The best time for travel is in your second trimester. You've caught your second wind – you're less tired, queasy and emotional – and you're not yet carrying a heavy load. Travel is rarely restricted during pregnancy unless there is a medical complication. But do get a green signal from your doctor first.

### 'Is it safe to travel long distance during pregnancy?'

Consider these factors and check with your doctor before making a decision to undertake any long-distance travel.

✓ How important is your trip?
✓ Will it be stressful?
✓ Can you take frequent loo breaks?
✓ Will you be able to maintain your diet?
✓ Will you get medical help should you need it?

Once you've been cleared for take off, do a little planning to ensure a safe and pleasant trip.

Time it right and choose a suitable, relaxing destination. Look up climate and weather conditions before your trip. Better yet, let your body set the itinerary. Remember, your safety and comfort come first.

## Never leave home without your pregnancy kit

Pack enough prenatal vitamins to last the trip and some healthy snacks. Carry comfortable clothes and shoes appropriate for your trip. Carry support hose if you think you will be sitting or standing for long periods.

*Food and drink:* Maintain your 'square meal' diet even on holiday. Remember your baby is growing and developing, so order carefully even as you enjoy local cuisine. Most importantly, eat regularly – 6 to 8 small meals a day. Consume bottled water, even when brushing your teeth. When you're away from home, it's better to stay safe.

*Move around:* Sitting for long periods can restrict circulation in your legs, so stretch, wriggle and massage your legs and feet as often as you can. Keep your feet elevated while you sit. Get up and walk around every hour. When travelling by car, make pit stops every couple of hours to stretch your legs.

*Flying the friendly skies:* Most airlines have rules regarding travelling in pregnancy and will not allow you to travel with them if you're 32 weeks and beyond. Book an aisle seat in front of the plane so that you're near the toilet and can move in and out easily. Be sure to carry snacks and drink plenty of fluids to counteract the dehydration caused by air travel. Wear your seatbelt below your belly.

If you're travelling across time zones, here are some tips to deal with jetlag:

✓   Ease yourself into the time zone. Set your watch and your schedule back or forward as needed. If you're heading east, start getting up a little earlier and going to bed a little earlier a few days before your departure. If you're heading west, go to bed a little later and get up a little later.

✓   Once you arrive at your destination, live on local time.

✓   Don't use any medicines without your doctor's approval.

## All aboard

Planning a train journey? Do your homework – check the train network and schedules. Make sure there's a dining car with a full menu. If not, carry your healthy meals and snacks. If you're travelling overnight, book a sleeper car – doing calisthenics in your chair seat is not the way to go. Besides, you don't want to start your trip worn out.

## Road trip

This is my favourite kind of holiday. Especially if you're not on any timetable and are prepared to take the scenic route to wherever it is you're going. Car travel also allows the most flexibility. You have room for all your personal belongings and you have control over when you stop and when you go. Keep a bagful of nutritious snacks and a thermos of juice or milk and plenty of water so you don't go hungry or thirsty. Be sure your seat is comfortable, keep a cushion for back support, wear your seatbelt and you're on your way!

# Pregnant Dads

'I had to carry my golf club for all 18 holes today. Honey, now I know exactly what you're going through.'

Paul Anka sang:

'You're having my baby...
What a lovely way of saying how much you love me.
Having my baby...
What a lovely way of saying what you're thinking of me.'

It is the ultimate compliment to a man when a woman decides to have his baby. It says that she is making a commitment to him and to the relationship by starting a family together. Why else would she be willing to subject herself to torture for nine months? She is going to suffer nausea, vomiting, aches and pains. She is going to swell up (literally!) and be short-tempered most of the time. She will be happy one minute and depressed the next.

I say to all you fathers-to-be: she is one brave woman and must love you a great deal! So, I ask you, why should she do this alone? If you love her (as I'm sure you do), buckle up because you are going to have the ride of your life for the next nine months.

As a father you have your own unique role to play in pregnancy. Although your physical work is done, your emotional work is just beginning. Think of it as a role-reversal, she's doing all the manual labour and you are providing emotional support for the next nine months. Consider this training for life as a dad!

Go to all the prenatal check-ups, read the pregnancy literature and share experiences like the baby's first kick. These are moments you will treasure forever.

## The first trimester

Pregnancy doesn't announce itself; it sneaks up on you – even if you've been planning it. Morning sickness and mood swings are probably the first signs you will notice. Her mood swings from one end of the spectrum to the other because of all the hormonal changes her body is going through. She could be happy and smiling one minute and angry as hell the next. The best way to deal with her erratic behaviour is to remember that this is all part of the 'pregnancy package' you've signed on for and not take it personally. After all, she is the one doing all the hard work, and trust me, it's hard!

Not only is she going through a lot physically, but emotionally too she is at her most vulnerable. So use this time wisely to help – not hinder – her progress. She needs all the love and support you can give. Help her with the chores; listen to her rave and rant. And above all, be ever ready with that back rub or foot massage or drives to get ice cream at 2 a.m.! Indulgence is the name of the game. Remember, happy moms make happy babies!

## The sex challenge

*What she feels:* If she's queasy and throwing up all the time, chances are she's not in the mood for sex or any kind of intimacy. She may also be insecure about her appearance or just awkward and clumsy as her body grows. On the other hand she might have a heightened sex drive due to the onslaught of pregnancy hormones.

*What you feel:* You too may be grappling with a similar range of emotions as the pregnancy progresses. It's called a fear of the unknown – you may worry about somehow hurting the baby during intercourse; or seeing your partner in new light, as a 'mother', might make you too nervous to make any overtures. Or perhaps you will find her physical transformation – she has new curves you've never seen before! – a highly sensual and exciting experience.

### So what should you do?

First of all, remember that this is only temporary and be extra sensitive and sympathetic to the physical demands on her body. Reassure her that she looks even more beautiful and be ever ready with a helping hand or the proverbial shoulder – in case she needs help with household chores or a good cry.

Pamper her with some extra TLC (tender loving care) if she's in the mood; cuddle up on the sofa while watching her favourite movie for the nth time. Use this time to bond, just the three of you – mom, dad and baby.

### Sympathy pains

Sympathetic pregnancy symptoms are called couvade and are fairly common. It's believed that up to 65 per cent of men experience at least one or more pregnancy symptoms during

their partner's pregnancy. Every time she rushes to throw up, you feel queasy too. You could also start experiencing backaches, gain weight and have trouble sleeping. The most likely cause is a combination of psychological, social and possibly even biological factors.

Use this opportunity to rest and recuperate together. Get a twin massage or enroll in couple's spa treatments. She needs pampering, why not you?

## The second trimester

She is now plum in the middle of her pregnancy, and feeling more aches and pains than you could imagine. Fortunately for you, you can't feel her physical discomfort but chances are you feel the brunt of her volatile emotions. Do you give her a wide berth when you feel a bad mood coming on? Find yourself making excuses to work late or going to the pub with your buddies? My advice: DON'T!

Your partner needs help and consideration right now, not avoidance. She needs you to understand her emotions, not shy away from them. Love and support her with your actions and you can make it through this pregnancy with an even stronger bond.

This is also a time when a little green monster rears its head – jealousy! Your partner is so engrossed in her pregnancy and baby that you may feel a little neglected. You are not alone – most men begin to feel a little left out at this stage.

To woo her again, do the little things you know will make her happy. Surprise her with flowers, take her out to dinner at her favourite restaurant, get away for the weekend. And never forget, as father-to-be, you have a vital role to play in this pregnancy: you are the pillar on which both mother and child depend.

## The third trimester

The countdown has begun, the pregnancy is drawing to a close. It's finally your time to play a more active role. You will be attending childbirth classes together. This means helping your partner through the hard work of labour and above all providing positive reinforcement and encouragement during delivery.

You've seen the scene played out enough times in movies – the woman screaming in pain and exhaustion, the man putting on a brave front, encouraging her to breathe and push... Yes, natural delivery can be a harrowing experience but when you finally get to cradle your baby in your arms for the very first time, it will all be worth it.

Johnny Depp said, 'Anything I've done up till May 27 1999 was kind of an illusion, existing without living. My daughter, the birth of my daughter, gave me life.'

Need I say more?

# And Finally

## Make love not war!

Sex is great therapy anytime but more so during your pregnancy. In fact, any type of TLC – cuddling on the sofa, holding hands, getting a back rub – can improve your mood and put a smile on your face.

You are going through a physical metamorphosis – some of it good – you are glowing and have curves in places you never imagined; and some of it not-so-good – you've put on weight and feel awkward and clumsy. You're probably looking for assurances from your husband/partner that he still desires you.

Sex or intimacy of any kind can give you the sense of well-being and self-confidence that you so desperately crave.

'My husband and I have always been extremely compatible in bed. But now, by the time we figure out what's safe and which position is most comfortable for my growing belly, all the passion has flown out the window! Why is it so complicated?'

Sex during pregnancy can be a daunting task to say the least. You could be concerned about safety and he could be worried about hurting the baby. Either way, romance does take a back seat. But don't be alarmed. Soon things will be back to normal.

In the meantime, try a little understanding, humour and a

bagful of patience and love, and you will overcome this challenge. Let's face it, things have changed. You're having a baby and like it or not, nothing's going to stay the same. Remember, it's the 'love' in lovemaking that is most important right now.

Talk about it openly and honestly with your partner. Ignoring the problem, if there is one, could lead to feelings of hurt, anger and frustration.

## The sexual rollercoaster

**In the first trimester**, many women find that sex is the last thing on their mind. Between all that nausea, vomiting and fatigue, it's hard to feel sexy.

But no two women or two pregnancies are alike, some of you may feel a surge of sexual desire. As a client of mine says, 'I loved what my pregnancy did for me... it gave me breasts! I felt gorgeous and sexy for the first time in my life!' You too might find that the first trimester makes you look sexier that you've ever looked before, thanks to your pregnancy hormones. Make the most of it.

**In the second trimester**, your libido could perk up a little, once the early pregnancy symptoms subside. Perhaps you feel less nauseous and more amorous. In fact, some women claim that sex during pregnancy was the best sex ever had! That's because extra blood flow to your sexual organs – the labia, clitoris and vagina – can make it easier to climax and to experience orgasms that are stronger and longer lasting, making lovemaking more pleasurable than ever.

And again, as we all know, nothing is set in stone during pregnancy. Some women lose all interest in sex in the second trimester. So if you're among the latter, relax! It's only temporary.

Sexual interest usually wanes again **in the third trimester**, as your body gets ready for delivery. You could find that your swollen belly makes sex extremely awkward now. Passion or romance is the last thing on your mind, especially since you're grappling with aches and pains and preparing for the baby's arrival.

The most important thing is to recognize that during pregnancy your sexual desires and those of your partner may not always be on the same wavelength. It's perfectly normal to want it one day and hate it the next. Rest assured, with a little understanding and communication and a lot of consideration and love, you're going to be just fine.

My simple guidelines for safe sex:

✓ Consult your doctor.
✓ Woman on top or lying on the side may be more comfortable as your pregnancy progresses.
✓ Understanding, consideration and humour will ensure smooth lovemaking.
✓ Say no if you're not in the mood.
✓ It is better to avoid intercourse after 36 weeks of pregnancy.

**Caution:** Intercourse is not advised for pregnant women who are experiencing preterm labour, premature cervical dilatation, or complications from a placental previa. Women with a twin pregnancy or a history of incompetent cervix and women at risk of premature delivery may also be advised to avoid intercourse.

## Childbirth classes

If you're a first-time parent, you're probably dreading the ordeal of childbirth. Sure, you've read about it, watched DVDs and heard all your friends' stories, but until you actually experience childbirth yourself, it's hard to imagine. This is exactly why I consider childbirth classes invaluable and recommend them to all my clients.

They are a good opportunity to focus on the impending experience, exchange pregnancy stories with other expectant couples, learn in depth about what to expect and how to cope with the intimidating process of delivery. At the very least you will learn a few breathing and relaxation exercises and coaching techniques, to prepare you for delivery.

A typical class consists of approximately 8 to 12 sessions and includes lectures and exercises led by a trained childbirth instructor. The classes emphasize the importance of diet and exercise during pregnancy, teach deep breathing techniques to manage pain and involve the husband/partner as an integral partner in the birth process.

You'll learn to recognize the signs of labour, when to call your doctor, when to go to the hospital, the logistics of labour and delivery, caesarean births, breastfeeding procedures and what to expect from your newborn.

### How it helps
*Relaxation*: As you begin to go into labour, the breathing techniques you have been taught will help you relax and manage your pain better.

*Understanding your body*: As your labour continues and you get closer to delivery, your connection and new-found understanding of your body lets you identify areas of tension. As you go into labour, certain positions will reduce the impact of your contractions and deepen your state of relaxation.

*Push!* When it's time to push, your muscles will work more effectively since the numerous squatting postures used during your prenatal classes, coupled with your heightened awareness, have strengthened your muscles months before the birth.

## Prenatal yoga

Prenatal yoga classes have become a popular choice with expectant mothers. The breathing techniques, awareness of the body, connection with the mind, modified postures and concentration have been known to aid in labour and delivery. Yoga is known to improve your focus and awareness. In delivery, this enhanced concentration can assist you during contractions, allowing you to concentrate on certain areas of the body and focus on relaxing these areas.

## The Lamaze technique

Pioneered by Dr Ferdinand Lamaze, Lamaze, also called the psycho prophylactic method, is one of the most common types of childbirth classes. The Lamaze philosophy of birth stipulates that 'birth is normal, natural and healthy'.

Lamaze uses knowledge and relaxation techniques to handle labour pain. It educates you so that when interventions are required, or pain relief medication is sought, you are able to make an informed choice.

It focuses on arming the expectant couple with various tools to ease discomfort and conserve energy in order to control pain as it occurs.

It encourages the use of deep breathing exercises and various 'distraction techniques' – like focusing on pleasant memories – as a way of distracting you from the pain of labour.

## The Bradley technique

In this approach, the father is assigned the role of 'coach' during the birthing process. It is his job to keep the mother focused on the task at hand, help with breathing exercises and provide plenty of reassurance and comfort.

The Bradley method uses deep abdominal breathing and encourages you to concentrate within and work with your body. These classes begin as soon as the pregnancy is confirmed and continue into the postpartum period in the belief that it takes a full nine months to get physically and emotionally prepared for labour and delivery.

It also includes advice on nutrition and diet for the mother during pregnancy and encourages regular exercise, so that you are properly trained to give birth.

### So which childbirth method should you choose?

I always recommend making an informed choice. Consult your doctor, examine your options and weigh the pros and cons of each method before deciding which childbirth class to attend. Choose the birthing method you're most comfortable with and which suits your needs best.

You need to have your baby your way!

## Waiting to exhale

'It's time!' After nine months of pain and planning, the moment is finally here – your baby's arrival. Here are some techniques to help you get ready for labour:

### Relaxation, deep breathing and visualization

These are alternative therapies that rely on breathing, muscle relaxation and guided imagery to develop a positive outlook to pregnancy and soothe the mind and body. Anxiety amplifies pain and slows labour. Conversely, relaxation diminishes the perception of pain and may improve the efficiency of your labour.

All this can help you safely through a variety of physical and emotional stresses during pregnancy from the miseries of morning sickness to the pain of labour and delivery. They can work wonders on general mother-to-be anxieties too.

## Drain the strain

Deep relaxation techniques, meditation and visualization can help you cope with a variety of physical and emotional stresses during pregnancy, enabling you to relax and focus your attention, reduce stress, lower your blood pressure and enhance your peace of mind. All of which you probably crave desperately right now.

## Deep breathing

Apart from getting a daily massage, one of the most effective ways to ease muscle tension, lower your heart rate and help you fall asleep is to breathe deeply and rhythmically.

Try this...

✓ Lie down on the floor or on your bed with your feet shoulder-width apart. (After the second trimester or if you're uncomfortable lying on your back, rest on your side with a pillow between your legs for support.)

✓ Breathe slowly through your nose, to the count of four, keeping your mouth closed. Be conscious of your stomach rising as you gradually fill your lungs and diaphragm with air. Then relax completely while exhaling through your nose slowly to the count of six or eight.

## Progressive muscle relaxation

This technique may take a couple of weeks to master, but once you do, you'll be glad you did. Think of it as a natural sleeping pill, which you'll really appreciate as your pregnancy progresses and a good night's sleep becomes more and more elusive.

Try this...

✓ Lie down on your bed or on the floor and tense all your muscles, then let them relax totally. Focus on one body part at a time. For example, start by tensing and releasing your face, chest, shoulders, arms, palms, stomach, hips, legs and finally, your feet and toes.

## Guided imagery

Remember when you were little and you got scared, your mom told you to close your eyes and think of happy things? Well, this is pretty similar.

Try this...

✓ Just picture yourself in a place you find peaceful or relaxing – a beach, a mountain top, or wherever your own private bliss may be. Next, imagine every detail of that place – the sounds, the smells, the colours.

Visualization takes some practice, but once you get the hang of it, it's a great way to quiet your mind, ease your tension and help you drift off to sleep.

# Happy Moms Make Happy Babies

Something must
be wrong;
I feel so good!

You're having a baby. There's no escaping the fact that you're going to feel the whole gamut of emotions – happy, sad, nervous, anxious, elated and depressed. You're also going to feel the whole gamut of physical symptoms – aches, pains, swelling and discomfort. It's the law of nature. So instead of wallowing in it, make the best of it!

Here's a reminder of the things happy mommies do:

## Make time for yourself

You deserve to take time off from your chores – put your feet up and enjoy a feel-good movie, read a book or listen to your favourite music.

'I am surrounded by people all day at work. When I get home all I want is some peace and quiet. I kick off my shoes, slip into my pyjamas and lie down for an hour. It feels great to do nothing!'

It's essential to unwind after a hectic day at home or at work. It's equally important to get some alone time. Go to your room, close the door and pretend you're alone on an island or on top of a mountain without a care in the world.

Trust me, everything else can wait!

## Make time for your friends

Your family can survive without you for a few hours, while you go out with your friends and just enjoy yourself.

'I would meet my friend for coffee at the corner coffee shop three days a week. We would talk, catch up on gossip or just do people watching. It got me out of the house, and for a while I forgot all my worries. It felt so good.'

Sometimes that's all it takes. Give yourself a break. You may be the one taking care of your family, but the sooner you make your family realize that your needs are just as important, the better. Remind them of the golden rule: when mother is happy, everyone is happy!

## The quick fix

Take 10 minutes to do absolutely nothing.

Close your eyes, breathe in slowly and deeply through your nose and exhale through your mouth. Repeat several times.

Think about a place you love and spend 10 minutes there in your mind.

**Learn to switch off**
Immerse yourself in any activity you find relaxing. Take up knitting, go window shopping for your baby, keep a journal, browse baby sites online, or walk it off – even a short stroll can be rejuvenating.

**Treasure the 'Kodak moments'**
Time flies when you're having babies and raising them. Preserve your pregnancy for posterity by making a time capsule. Treasure all those happy moments: the first ultrasound, her dad talking to her inside your belly, even the snack you craved at midnight. Years from now, when your baby is old enough to understand, she'll enjoy seeing things the way they were before she arrived.

One client recalls, 'I was expecting twins and miscarried one in my second month. When my baby was older I told her that she was one of twins and her first question to me was, "Which one did you want?" I hugged her close and said, "The one I got!" Had I taken photographs of myself in my third month lying in bed with my legs propped up on pillows (I was advised bed rest to avoid a second miscarriage), I would have been able to show her how hard I fought to keep her!'

It is equally important for your child to realize what you endured to have her. Trust me, this will only strengthen the bond you formed while she was in your womb.

Finally, remember that your stress quotient is only going to increase once your baby is born. So it makes sense to find ways to handle it better or bring it down to a manageable level now. Besides, when you finally hold your little bundle of joy in your arms, all the stress and pain will be a distant memory.

Someone once said, 'A baby will make love stronger, days shorter, nights longer, bankroll smaller, home happier, clothes shabbier, the past forgotten and the future worth living for.'

So sit back, take a deep breath and relax. You have everything to look forward to. Good luck and happy parenting!

# Bibliography

Anthony, L. *Pre and Post-Natal Fitness: A Guide for Fitness Professionals from the American Council on Exercise*, Monterey, CA: Healthy Learning, 2002.

Barbieri, R.L. and J.T. Repke. 'Medical Disorders during Pregnancy' in D.L. Kasper, E. Braunwald, A.S. Fauci, S.L. Hauser, D.L. Longo, J.L. Jameson and J. Loscalzo (eds), *Harrison's Principles of Internal Medicine*, 16th edition, New York: McGraw-Hill, 2008, pp. 32–38.

Catanzaro, R. and R. Artal. 'Physical Activity and Exercise in Pregnancy' in C.J. Lammi-Keefe, S.C. Couch and E.H. Philipson (eds), *Handbook of Nutrition and Pregnancy*, Totowa, NJ: Humana Press, 2008, pp. 37–53.

Cheskin, L.J. 'Special Populations' in R. T. Cotton and C. J. Ekeroth (eds), *ACE Lifestyle & Weight Management Consultant Manual*, pp 248–63, CA: Healthy Learning, 1996, pp. 248–63.

Church, T. 'General Overview of Preparticipation Health Screening and Risk Assessment', *American College of Sports Medicine Resource Manual for Guidelines for Exercise Testing and Prescription*, 5th edition, Baltimore: Lippincott Williams & Wilkins, 2006, pp. 115–22.

Colleen Stainton, M. and E.J. Ann Nef. 'Wrist Bands Control Nausea and Vomiting in Pregnancy', *Women's Health*, 1995, p. 63.

Davies, G.A.L., C. Maxwell and L. McLeod. 'Obesity in Pregnancy', *SOGC Clinical Practice Guidelines*, No. 239, 2010.

Davis, M. 'Nausea and Vomiting of Pregnancy – An Evidence-based Review', *Journal of Perinatal Neonatal Nursing*, Vol. 18, No. 4, 2004, pp. 312–28.

Dundee, J.W., F.B.R. Sourial, R.G. Ghaly and P.F. Bell. 'Acupressure Reduces Morning Sickness', *Journal of Royal Society of Medicine*, Vol. 81, 1988, pp. 456–7.

Dutta, D.C. 'Physiological Changes during Pregnancy' in H. Konar (ed), *Textbook of Obstetrics*, 6th edition, Calcutta: New Central Book Agency, 2004, pp. 46–56.

Entin, P.L. and K.M. Munhall. 'Recommendations Regarding Exercise During Pregnancy Made By Private/Small Group Practice Obstetricians in the USA', *Journal of Sports Science and Medicine*, Vol. 5, 2006, pp. 449–58.

Erick, M. 'Nutrition during Pregnancy and Lactation' in L. K. Mahan, S. Escott-Stump (eds), *Krause's Food & Nutrition Therapy*, 12th edition, St Louis: Saunders Elsevier, 2008, pp. 160–98.

Fell, D.B., K.S. Joseph, B.A. Armson and L. Dodds. 'The Impact of Pregnancy on Physical Activity Level', *Journal of Maternal and Child Health*, 2008.

Harrison, C.L., R.G. Thompson, H.J.Teede and C.B. Lombard. 'Measuring physical activity during pregnancy', *International Journal of Behavioral Nutrition and Physical Activity*, Vol. 8, 2011, p. 19.

Hegaard, H. K., H. Kjaergaard, P.P. Damm, K. Petersson, A.K. Dykes. 'Experiences of physical activity during pregnancy in Danish nulliparous women with a physically active life before pregnancy: a qualitative study', *BMC, Pregnancy and Childbirth*, Vol. 10, 2010, p. 33.

Hyatt, G. and C.Cram. *Prenatal & Post Partum Exercise Design*, Tucson: D.S.W. Fitness, 2003.

Koch, K.L., R.M. Stern, M. Vasey, J.J.Botti, G.W.Creasy, G.W., and A. Dwyer. 'Gastric Dysrhythmias and Nausea of Pregnancy', *Digestive Diseases and Sciences*, Vol. 35, No. 8, 1990, pp. 961–68.

W.D. McArdle, F.I. Katch, and V.L. Katch 'Training for Anaerobic and Aerobic Power', *Exercise Physiology, Energy, Nutrition and Human Performance*, 5th edition, Maryland: Lippincott Williams & Wilkins, 2001, pp. 458–99.

Murphy Goodwin, T. 'Nausea and Vomiting of Pregnancy', *OBG Management*, 2004, pp. 54-67.

Pepper, G.V. and S.C. Roberts. 'Rates of Nausea and Vomiting in Pregnancy and Dietary Characteristics across Populations', *The Royal Society*, Vol. 273, 2006, pp. 2675–79.

Rafla, N., M.S. Nair, S. Kumar. 'Exercise in Pregnancy' in J. Studd, S. L. Tan, F. A. Chervenak (eds), *Progress in Obstetrics and Gynecology*, Vol. 18, London: Elsevier, 2009, pp. 29–46.

Roberts, S. 'Special Populations and Health Concerns' in C. X. Bryant, D. J. Green (eds), *American Council On Exercise Personal Trainer Manual*, 3rd edition, San Diego, CA: American Council on Exercise, 2003, pp. 345-369.

Royal College of Obstetricians and Gynaecologists, 'Exercise in Pregnancy', *RCOG, Statement* No. 4, 2006.

Schlüssel, M.M., E. Bicalho de Souza, M.E. Reichenheim, G. Kac. 'Physical Activity during Pregnancy and Maternal-Child Health Outcomes: A Systematic Literature Review', Cad. Saúde Pública, Rio de Janeiro, 24 Sup 4, 2008, pp. S531-S544.

Schramm, W.F., J.W. Stockbauer, J.H. Hoffman. 'Exercise, Employment, Other Daily Activities, and Adverse Pregnancy Outcomes', *American Journal of Epidemiology*, Vol. 143, No. 3, 1996, pp. 211-18.

Sorensen, T.K., M.A. Williams, I.M. Lee, E.E. Dashow, M.L. Thompson, D.A. Luthy. 'Recreational Physical Activity during Pregnancy and Risk of Preeclampsia', *Hypertension*, Vol. 41, 2003, pp. 1273–80.

Srilakshmi, B. 'Nutritional and Food Requirements for Expectant Mothers', *Dietetics*, 5th edition, New Delhi: New Age International (P) Limited, 2009, pp. 88–102.

Wang, T.W. and B.S. Apgar. 'Exercise during Pregnancy', *American Academy of Family Physicians*, 1998.

Wolfe, L.A., and G.A.L. Davies, 'Canadian Guidelines for Exercise in Pregnancy', *Clinical Obstetrics and Gynecology*, Vol. 46, No. 2, 2003, pp. 488–95.

Wygand, J.W. and K.M. Cahill. 'Exercise Programming', *American College of Sports Medicine Certification Review*, 2nd edition, Baltimore: Lippincott Williams & Wilkins, 2006, pp. 154–71.

# Acknowledgements

I am extremely grateful for the encouragement and support of these important people without whom this book would not have been possible.

Dr R. P. Soonawala – for his helpful guidance and for graciously agreeing to write the foreword. His kindness has helped give my book the credibility it needs.

My publisher HarperCollins – the editorial team, in particular my editor Neelini Sarkar for her valuable insights and suggestions during the process.

My creative consultant Anita Bakshi – for sieving through my notes and assisting me in collating the reams of information available on this exhaustive subject.

And finally my clients and patients – for their 'real life' stories and experiences which gave me the inspiration and impetus to carry this baby to term.